DOGS WITH NO NAMES

In Pursuit of Courage, Hope and Purpose

Published by Meerkat Media 2012

Dogs with No Names – In Pursuit of Courage, Hope and Purpose may be purchased at special discount for bulk purchases and
fundraising through www.dogswithnonames.ca or Meerkat Media, Box 1040, Bragg Creek, AB, T0L 0K0, Canada.

Library and Archives Canada Cataloguing in Publication

Samson, Judith, 1960-
Dogs with no names : in pursuit of courage, hope and
purpose / Judith Samson-French.

Includes bibliographical references.
ISBN 978-0-9917240-0-0

1. Feral dogs--Alberta--Tsuu T'ina Nation 145. I. Title.

SF810.7.D65S36 2012   636.7'0832   C2012-906469-6

Designed by Sue Impey, By Design Desktop Publishing Inc.

Front and back cover photos by Evocative Photography

Printed in Canada on FSC paper.

DOGS WITH NO NAMES

In Pursuit of Courage, Hope and Purpose

Judith Samson-French DVM

One hundred percent of the profits from the sale of this book will be donated to the *Dogs with No Names* project.

"The compassion and determination that shine through each page of this wonderful book provide a compelling reminder of our deep connections to all other living things and of the potential that resides within each and every one of us to make change in the world."

Jane Lawton, CEO, Jane Goodall Institute of Canada

Contents

Author's Note

Even when we can't see them, we know they are there. On occasion, we hear them howling on cold winter nights, in short sequence like coyotes do. Sometimes in the light of day we catch a glimpse of them limping along the ditch, tongues hanging out, trotting to unknown destinations. They seem to be in a place where only the present matters, oblivious to their surroundings. Their eyes tell us that yesterday is forgotten and tomorrow does not yet exist. They are the dogs with no names, and they roam the reserve lands of North America. There are millions of them. They are unwanted, and they know it.

I have come into contact with many of them in my surgery suite, where their broken legs needed mending and porcupine quills needed to be removed from their faces. Fortunately for them, they had this in common: they were too weak to resist capture and restraint by the good people who went out of their way to pick them up. Without exception, once healed, none of these dogs returned to their lives of freedom and mortal perils. Each was given a name, a collar, and a loving home.

Prior to working with dogs with no names, I ensured I was properly vaccinated for tetanus and rabies. Some of them, I thought, might decide to convey their displeasure at being handled by sinking their teeth into my flesh. I was wrong. After working as a doctor of veterinary medicine with companion dogs for over twenty years, I realized how little I knew about canines until I included these dogs in my practice.

They taught me what the true essence of a dog really is. I had to reconsider their tremendous potential, and the severe limitations we unknowingly impose on them while they accompany us on our life journeys. Every moment spent in a dog's company is enriching; every step taken alongside them is lighter. There is so much more to discover from this alliance. It is my hope that by engaging yourself in the stories of *Dogs with No Names*, you will perceive dogs, and our bond with them, in a new light.

Judith Samson-French

To all dogs that need a helping hand

Introduction

The root of the feral dog problem

Many among us assume that the hordes of free-roaming dogs on reserves are feral, neglected, and potentially dangerous; that people inhabiting reserves are callous and uncaring as far as domestic animals are concerned; and that the dog overpopulation is their fault and therefore their problem. Such assumptions are generally made by those who have never set foot on this land. True enough, on the reserve side of the border, animal concerns are, for the most part, perceived and handled differently than what we are used to in our urban society. But the underlying problem with dogs on reserve land is the same throughout the world: there are too many unwanted dogs. Because of uncontrolled and uncontrollable breeding of dogs, the population remains excessively high. Compounding the problem is the absence of municipal animal shelters and resources. And to make matters worse, there is an influx of dogs abandoned by people from outside the reserves. Maybe they think the creatures dumped here will have a second chance. *They rarely do.*

Through domestication, all dogs have lost the genetic impetus to breed only once a year, as their wolf relatives still do – in the spring when food and water are more plentiful and the conditions favourable. Instead, dogs can produce litters of eight to sixteen puppies nearly twice a year. Such fertility quickly outpaces the number of homes available to care for them. Not surprisingly, most of these excess dogs are considered pests, foraging in garbage bins and dumps; digging dens under buildings; and displaying aggressive behaviours around puppies and females in heat, and while defending their food sources and territories. They also carry parasites, and sometimes diseases such as rabies. Many of these unwanted dogs, driven away from human habitations with threatening yells, waving shovels, and even gunshots, have learned to live elusive lives. Unable to hunt efficiently, however, they need discarded food to survive, forcing them to live within range of humans. Many live in a completely feral state, irreversibly fearful of humans, seen but never touched, furtively slinking about, always on the fringe. Others live in a semi-feral state, tolerating some human contact, perhaps even desiring it. But without positive, sustained social interaction with humans before the age of sixteen weeks, these dogs are destined to remain forever fearful of humans.

Why hasn't something been done?

One of our basic human drives is to avoid discomfort. We've all resorted to avoidance and denial when confronted with distressing realities, and tried to distance ourselves from uncomfortable situations. This normal coping mechanism has one major drawback: the problem causing the internal conflict is never examined and thus never resolved. And so the painful and overwhelming reality remains: in all Canadian provinces and most states of the US that are home to First Nations reserves, millions of unwanted dogs roam unchecked, scratching out a living as best they can. The majority exist on the edge of society, neither belonging to people nor capable of living without them. They are often referred to simply as "rez dogs."*

*The term "rez dog" is used without prejudice in this book.

A new solution to an old dilemma

Because most dogs are sexually mature at six months and successfully produce at least two live puppies as their own replacements, the population cycle never ebbs. The presence of so many unwanted dogs often presents a high nuisance factor to society. For our sake as well as theirs, the world would undoubtedly be a better place without them. Realistically, we may never be able to make feral dogs disappear entirely. But can we not at least reduce their numbers and the suffering they endure?

Currently, the only humane and socially acceptable approach to solving the overpopulation crisis of unwanted dogs is contraception. In affluent societies, surgical sterilization – spaying female dogs and neutering male dogs – has been used extensively in the last two decades to control the numbers of unwanted dogs. In many places, however, this approach is impractical for obvious reasons: the prohibitive cost of surgery, the paucity of veterinary surgeons, and the restricted access to necessary drugs. But there is another solution: contraception without surgery. Although contraceptive implants are widely used in North American zoos to control reproduction of their animal stock, their use as a means of controlling fertility in unwanted dogs has never been tried before.

The "dogs with no names" project

Without adequate food, water, and shelter available to them, most rez dogs do not have a life worth living, at least not by any human standard. This is especially true in northern climates with severe winter conditions. While adoptions of rez dogs are possible and encouraged through rescue groups, they are unfortunately limited to younger pups and tamer dogs that can make the transition to life as a companion dog. Adoption of truly feral and semi-feral dogs is fraught with difficulties, if not impossible, due to the fearful nature of most and the shortage of welcoming

homes. It was with the hope of reducing the suffering of dogs left homeless on reserves that the "dogs with no names" venture was born. This innovative pilot project offers a potential solution to the dog overpopulation problem: the use of contraceptive implants to prevent unwanted dogs from being born in the first place.

The procedure is quick and requires minimal handling. The implant, injected under the skin of a female dog, is painless when given with local freezing, doesn't require extensive technical skills, and presents no ill side effects. Of course, there are still challenges: you must first catch the dogs, cost is a concern (although only about one-third the cost of spay surgery), and the implant confers infertility on a temporary basis only – about eighteen months.* Sadly, the short lifespan of the implant has not been a significant issue, as many rez dogs do not outlive the duration of the implant, and even fewer live long enough to receive the two implants required up to the age of three years.

*In a perfect world, a one-time injection would be given to dogs (and cats) of either sex to produce instant infertility. The good news is that scientists are working on precisely that solution: it is a tall order, probably achievable but likely decades away in its application.

The result

Through the contraceptive project, we have successfully implanted over 100 female dogs and, when figures are compounded over forty months, prevented the birth of over 100,000 puppies. Although we initiated this process with the hope of doing just that, much more has emerged as a result of it.

Thanks to this innovation, bridges have been built with First Nations community members, and a deeper understanding of the true essence of our companion dogs has come to light. But the best gift of all was an unintended consequence: the wealth of lessons learned from the "dogs with no names."

This book was written to honour the enduring bond between dog and man and the unfaltering alliance our best friends made with us.

Pregnant Pause Concept

Sometimes the way we think is part of the problem.
Our challenge now is to think outside the box.

Millions of dogs are destroyed every year in North America. And worldwide, the overpopulation of dogs is epidemic. Some estimates go as high as 600 million. Imagine: *600 million.*

Overall, society's approach to the overpopulation of dogs has been focused on surgical sterilization, along with the killing of surplus animals. These attempts have seen mixed results at best, and repeated failures at worst. Surgical sterilization of dogs on reserves, albeit an important component of population control when dealing with "owned" dogs, has failed miserably at reducing populations of feral and semi-feral dogs. Nor has mass killing of these dogs proven effective, at least not as a long-term solution.

Sometimes the way we think is part of the problem. Our challenge now is to think outside the box. If spay surgery is not a feasible option for female dogs – for whatever reason – could they at least be provided with a "pregnant pause"? The simple answer comes in a tiny white tube manufactured in Australia, a contraceptive implant already used to prevent breeding among captive wild animals in North American zoos. The product, having undergone extensive research, seemed a realistic option for the reserve dogs. Once we completed and filed the appropriate forms with the Canadian government, the implants were made available for use on an emergency drug release permit.

One obvious shortfall remained: though state of the art, the implant suppressed reproduction for only about 18 months, at which time another implant would be necessary to prolong sterilization. Sadly, we discovered that the expiry date was hardly a problem: nearly 50 per cent of the females implanted in our study group were either never seen again or did not survive longer than 12 months beyond receiving their implants. Our success in preventing multiple litter births during that short time was undeniably good news, yet the downside was disturbingly clear: for dogs on the rez, life was harsher than we had ever imagined. Yes, capturing and implanting the wilder females had its challenges – but preventing life from beginning was still *a much less desperate act than terminating it*. Less desperate, too, than witnessing the premature, anguished deaths of these homeless animals who deserve so much more from us.

In theory, over 100,000 puppies are not born thanks to the use of contraceptive implants in 100 female dogs over a 40 month period. Here are the numbers: a female dog (let's call her Granny) can give birth to 8 puppies before a year of age. Assuming that 4 of those are females, they will each in turn give birth to another 8 puppies before Granny gives birth to her second litter of 8 pups at 2 years of age. At that time Granny's next 4 female puppies will each give birth to another 8 puppies while her daughters and grand-daughters give birth to another 8 puppies and so on and so on…

...for dogs on the rez, life was harsher than we had ever imagined.

Rez Dogs 101

Dog #27 — found at site 6 on 06/27/11

"Rez Dog: An informal term for outdoor, stray, and feral dogs living on Indian reservations in the United States and Canada."

– Wikipedia Encyclopedia

Physical Characteristics:

- 99% have no collar, tag, microchip or tattoo

- Usually a mid-size dog – too big… hard to get enough to eat; too small…hard to keep from being eaten

- Often with medium to long hair in order to survive the winter

- Coat is usually shiny even with a lack of food (not certain why)

- Color is usually black with tan, rarely white or spotted colors; dominant gene and nature's preference

- Tail, ears and testicles are intact – no docking or neutering

- If female, will be bred at every cycle – 6 months

- May have scars, particularly on face and ears

Note:
Generally these dogs can be sorted into two categories:
- Dogs with a name may be owned companion dogs
- Dogs with no names are semi-feral (tolerate some human contact) or feral

Unless irreversibly fearful of humans, many rez dogs, once they feel a kind hand, hear a soft voice, and perceive patience in the gaze of a human's eyes, offer their loyalty in return. It is their nature to please and be accepted.

Behaviour:

- Territorial with resources such as females, food and space

- May be solitary or live in loosely structured packs

- Usually behaves in a submissive way with humans; life depends on it

- May display strong fight or flight characteristics

- Adept at scavenging and will eat most anything – not an efficient hunter

- Knows how to dig and how to den, like wolves

- Does not know that the only good time of the year to have pups is the spring (unlike wolves)

- If need be, is cannibalistic, and incest is not a bother

- Adaptable and resilient

- Does not respond to "sit"; just looks quizzical and walks away

Health:

- Life expectancy often depends on residency status – most feral dogs don't enjoy a long life

- Male has a longer life expectancy; female has many more demands upon her body

- Guts are home to many parasites (hard on them when food in short supply)

- Fur can be home to fleas and mites

- May carry rabies, parvovirus, distemper

Residency:

- May be certain – they live at or near a particular house, or in question – may have a territory in neighbourhood or out on the fringe

- Almost all have freedom to roam

- Aggressive disputes with other dogs over home range not unusual

- A pup's initial home is often under a deck, in an abandoned house, or in the forest

The Price of Freedom

" Our freedom can be measured by the
number of things we can walk away from."

-Vernon Howard

For a dog
freedom is not
free, it has a
price, death.

Mortal Perils

Simply surviving to see a new day is a victory for rez dogs, since many do not. This female dog was found lying dead on the grass near the side of a road, most likely hit by a car. Some kind soul had deliberately placed a blanket over her. Although later blown off by the relentless prairie wind, the blanket – for a while at least – hid the dog's lifeless body from view and prevented further disfigurement from pecking ravens.

There were houses nearby, and children playing only a few yards away from where the dog lay rigid – a demoralizing sight that would remain until other dogs, coyotes and birds had finished scavenging what they could from the carcass and dragged the bones away.

Unlike dogs owned by city dwellers, rez dogs face many unique challenges in their struggle for survival. A lack of the necessary resources to sustain life, such as food, water and shelter, is obviously paramount. Out here, the risk of encounters with other potentially mortal perils looms larger as well. These free roaming dogs repeatedly interact with mostly intact, unvaccinated, and sometimes desperate members of their own species. This alone adds a whole host of threats to their short lives.

Most rez dogs naturally roam in search of resources. Intact males are further motivated by reproductive urges and will travel miles from their home range, hoping to catch the scent of a female. They will traverse dangerous and unfamiliar ground, across roads and woodlands, risking confrontation with vehicles, wildlife, other dogs and even humans in their single-minded quest.

The female dog contributes to these events by giving off pheromones signaling her "receptive" status when in heat. She attracts many wandering males who will attempt to possess her and breed her. Competing would-be suitors will fight for dominance, often viciously. Such is the inevitable pattern, averted only in the unlikely event that the female is locked away for three weeks of every six-month cycle.

Dog #38 had 3 pups —
later rescued

Consensual Sex

Among feral dogs, primal urges rule. What we see here is consensual sex, driven solely by natural hormonal surges and responses. This black chow-type female dog has become a prized possession for the black male dog, and he guards her fiercely. No other male dogs dare approach this sexually receptive female. If one is reckless enough to make a move, he can expect a blast of overt aggression from the black male, starting with a full-blown lip curl and a threatening growl. If the offender persists, her defender will snap to an alert standing posture, his tail fully erect. How much further would he go to protect his trophy? This we were unable to discern, for one simple reason: not a single male dog challenged him any further. But after repeated breeding by the black male, the female failed to produce the expected litter two months later.

When we spotted her eight months later, however, on a cold, windy late winter day, the chow female was nursing three young puppies. She had them hidden in a den dug four feet underground, beneath the deck of a house. No blankets, no heat, no light.

On that blustery day, we coaxed the female out and implanted her with a contraceptive. To prevent further physical debilitation of their mother, we collected the three puppies from their underground den and found them safe refuge in a foster home. They would likely have died otherwise, considering the lack of available water. The same black male, we noticed, was still around. From the puppies' black and silver markings, we had little doubt he was the father of the brood, but this time, the fickle male paid no attention to the nursing female; she was not in heat and barely worth a passing glance.

> "Life is a sexually transmitted disease."
>
> – R. D. Laing

In the case of the winter-born puppies, we were grateful that the occupant of the house let us take the three puppies for adoption, especially since two of them were males. Had they stayed, we can predict the dismal scenario that would likely unfold. Two or three months after they stop nursing, the pups would reach puberty (usually any time over five months of age). At that stage, full-blown sibling rivalry would ensue, with both male pups bent on breeding their mother and sister. In a "winner takes all" showdown, the victor would claim his prizes, successfully breeding his mother and sister. And the loser? Well, he'd be left licking the bite wounds inflicted by his testosterone-fueled brother. Indeed, domesticated dogs have lost all biological barriers to incestuous interaction with family members.

What exactly is the problem with incest among dogs? From a strictly biological stance, incest preserves and compounds the effects of "bad" genes in a gene pool. To shed some light on the dangers of incest, let's take a moment here for a quickie course in genetics: DNA, the blueprint of life, is divvied up into two sets of 39 chromosomes each, for a total of 78 in a normal dog. One set of 39 comes from the father, while the other comes from the mother. Let's say a dog gets a bad gene from the mother – blindness as in progressive retinal atrophy, for instance. If the father's copy of that gene is normal, then the good version acts as a backup, effectively preventing blindness from being passed on. But if the blind dog breeds with its sibling, the chances of getting two copies of the blindness gene rise drastically when compared to coupling with another dog without the close genetic linkage. When each sibling has a copy of the bad eye gene, the offspring from such breeding have an increased chance of *not* inheriting a normal copy. Here's where our ignorance about selective breeding can magnify the problem and wreak havoc. Imagine multiplying the effect of bad genes – such as the blindness gene – by any other deleterious genes sprinkled among an estimated 25,000 to 35,000 active genes in dogs. What do you get? Without question, some life-shortening or quality altering problems are bound to arise.

Why do dogs not imitate the behavior of their wild counterpart, the wolf, and avoid inbreeding at all costs? Here's the short answer: because they can't. Domestication by well-meaning humans has severely impaired the dog's natural response for survival. This happens with all domesticated species. A rooster, for example, will breed indiscriminately with his daughters; a stallion will impregnate his sister; a ewe will allow her son to mount her; and a cow will let her brother do the same. Unfortunately, letting domesticated animals revert to a feral state will not reverse this life-hindering reproductive process, not in our lifespan anyway. On the contrary, feral animals suffer more because of their inability to change their human-altered genetic blueprint and face natural selective pressures on their own.

Unable to catch these littermates, the brother bred with his sister

Doing nothing for those who can't defend themselves is not tolerance but apathy. Tolerance is a virtue, apathy a sin.

Sixteen Embryos

Under the surgical drape, breathing anesthetic gas, a female dog lies unmoving under the surgeon's probing hands. This slumbering patient has long been a vagabond on the reserve. When found, she was very thin with an enlarged abdomen and mildly developed mammary glands, the likely signs of a pregnancy. Her previous litter, born early in the fall in a crude dirt depression dug under a spruce tree, did not fare well: out of a dozen puppies, only two survived. Those two became vagabonds themselves, scavenging for food like all the others. Finally, in January, starving and weak, the bedraggled female dog was caught and brought in for spay surgery. During the procedure, we discover sixteen embryos, smaller than the size of golf balls, in in her uterus. If they're left to grow undisturbed, her babies will likely be born in another three or four weeks, in the worst of winter conditions.

This female dog with no name and no home has been cursed with the worst luck in the canine world: sixteen embryos developing, and no

sixteen golfball size embyos in this uterus

steady source of food to supply enough protein, calcium and phosphorus to build up all the little bodies growing inside her. If the pregnancy continues, by the time the little ones are due to emerge from their mother's protective womb, temperatures will be well into the sub-zero range. Although there is likely more than one father for this litter, none will have the paternal instinct to help this female provide food for the puppies. Worse yet, nature's odds are stacked against the survival of so many infants: with only twelve mammary glands and nipples to nourish all of them, four puppies will be forced to go hungry at each feeding. The mother's health is at risk too: an extensive litter like this requires an incredibly energy draining lactation period, one that will likely cost the female her life – and with it, the lives of each of these puppies. To be a dog with no name can be a cruel fate.

If you passed this vagabond female on the reserve, would you think it best to leave her be, and let nature take its course? Would you resist the urge to pick her up, convincing yourself that to do so would be interfering in something that does not concern you? If you were the surgeon, would you remove the embryo-filled uterus, reminding yourself that the world has no need for more homeless dogs? Or would you decide not to proceed with the spaying and destruction of these embryos, out of respect for all life forms?

How much should we concern ourselves with suffering inflicted on others, if it is not our doing and we have no responsibility for it? With all the valid reasons we have to appease our collective conscience by turning a blind eye and making no attempt to ease the suffering around us, why bother to do anything at all? The answer is simple. Because when we try to rationalize our reasons for doing nothing, we create an even larger problem. Indeed, we put ourselves in danger of losing a slice of our humanity that cannot be regained.

surgery notes —
dorsal recumbency, IV LRS
@ 10ml/kg/hr, starting spO$_2$
95 pulse 98, incision along linea
alba, no peritoneal fat,
ovaries intact with pregnant
uterus...

44

Failing at Family Planning

Rez dogs, sadly, fail miserably at family planning according to nature's intended cycle, and the penalty is harsh. The will to live or die depends largely on the time of the year a dog is born. A birth late in the fall or winter heralds gloom for a litter of pups born into harsh elements. In the cold, the odds of puppies making it to adulthood (beyond six months of age) are estimated at a dismal 1 in 7. Although a mother will have taxed her own energy reserves to produce seven foetuses, she will likely still give birth to seven healthy puppies. But adversity hits hard immediately after birth when lactation is triggered: milk production exerts a tremendous energy drain on the mammalian body, far greater than pregnancy. Unfortunately for the mother, there is no sharing of parental duties; the burden of feeding herself and her litter is exclusively her privilege and her duty. No doubt driven by strong instincts, she will accomplish this with impeccable devotion. Even though her body condition will be dangerously close to fatal emaciation, she will offer her mammary glands to her offspring, and they will feed ravenously and selfishly. They will be plump and she will be thin. In time, they will be thin and she will be skeletal.

Despite their failure at family planning, rez dogs are in little danger of becoming extinct, since survival of a species depends only on the parents producing two live offspring in their lifetime. In reality, these dogs fulfill that mandate not in a lifespan, but every year. Each female produces nearly two litters a year, one in the colder months, when only the hardiest among the puppies may be lucky enough to survive; and another in the warmer months, when seven puppies or more may survive to breed. For these unwanted dogs, the relentless cycle will continue unabated unless external forces launch either a massive adoption program or a massive contraception program, or both. Unfortunately, many truly feral dogs will be excluded from both programs, and this unlucky oversight will perpetuate the births of outcasts.

For these unwanted dogs, the relentless cycle will
continue unabated unless external forces launch
either a massive adoption program or a massive
contraception program, or both.

The Singleton Life

All too often, harsh conditions wipe out the most vulnerable of the puppies born in the wild. In late winter and early spring, the sight of a singleton seeking refuge under an old disused vehicle is not uncommon. Likely he is the lone survivor of an unfortunate litter born during the fall or winter. So far he has beat the odds by managing to stay alive into the spring, perhaps alongside his mother. Or perhaps not; like his absent siblings, she too may have succumbed to the lack of food, water and shelter. But the singleton's life is still in immediate danger: without brothers or sisters to interact and socialize with, this lone dog has no opportunity to learn the crucial lessons of appropriate canine body language and behaviours. Indeed, this clumsy male is at risk of unforgiveable social blunders. What if he makes the wrong eye contact or adopts the wrong body posture, at the wrong time and with the wrong dog? Such a gaffe could result in fatal bite wounds.

Nor would he likely fare any better in human circles. Deprived of people contact, the singleton remains hopelessly inept at reading human body language, and may never be eligible for adoption due to his poor social skills. Essentially, he is doomed to lead a life on the fringe, one day at a time. His lifespan will likely be counted in months, not years.

A puppy born in the spring or summer, conversely, has a much better chance for a longer life. The bitch will likely have an easier time finding water, and will not expend as much energy trying to stay warm herself. Fair-weather puppies will typically

maintain a heavier body weight, and their survival rate to adulthood can easily reach 50 to 100 percent, depending on whether or not scavenging for food is an easy task. At the very least, food and water – when found – are not frozen solid.

Warm-season birthdays offer another bonus: because of the larger number of live puppies per litter, proper socialization is more likely to take place. The pups will learn to interact appropriately with littermates and other dogs, thereby reducing the threat of aggression and cannibalism. Socialization with humans is also more likely to occur, as the pups will be able to travel longer distances in clement weather in their search for water, food and companionship, and such excursions increase their odds of meeting a diverse range of people. Of course, more extensive travel increases their odds of encountering mortal perils as well. Safety and security are tenuous at best for dogs living on the edge.

Always Thirsty

With September here and chillier days warning of winter's imminent approach, this industrious dog is checking one of his last fresh water points. About two inches of shallow muddy water sit at the bottom of this blue receptacle, and it has already been touched by frost. As we watch, the dog pounds twice with his front feet to break the thin ice, and then slurps down a long, loud drink. Is he able to sense the harsh days ahead? These drinks will become fewer and farther between as below-freezing temperatures become a certainty. And at some point they will disappear altogether.

She might look sheepish at being caught in the act, but this clever dog has learned a key survival tactic: how to stay hydrated. When the horses are at the far end of the corral, she cautiously trots over to the stock waterer and helps herself to an ample drink. Unfortunately, her situation is more the exception

Dehydration, not starvation,
often causes their demise.

than the norm, as horse owners are few in this area, and stock waterers even fewer. Dehydration is a life-threatening problem for any reserve dogs that cannot regularly access water bowls – and most of them fit this category. While water might be provided on a regular basis for some fortunate dogs, this again is the exception and not the rule. As such, a bucket of water

may be an infrequent find, and when it is available, it disappears quickly. Thirsty animals make for high demand and tough competition. And in sub-zero temperatures, any water provided takes only minutes to freeze and become useless – leaving the dogs even more desperate.

To make matters worse, any natural sources of water nearby are also frozen in the cold months, and usable only when temperatures climb. By summertime, the spring runoff has long since dried up. So for the majority of the year, a reliable water supply for the dogs is scarce. For a bitch to get enough water to sustain lactation, she needs to find a regular water source. Any available livestock water troughs are a blessing for her and her babies. The biggest challenge comes once the mother has weaned her puppies: if they are eating snow for hydration, the little ones will not have enough body fat to prevent them from becoming hypothermic. And if snow is unavailable, they might be too small to trot alongside their mother to seek water elsewhere, or too small to reach the supply if one is indeed found. Dehydration, not starvation, often causes their demise.

Many kind people help to provide food for rez dogs, which is an incredible life-saving gesture, particularly in winter. However, free flowing water is as critical as food to the dog's survival – during any time of the year. And no matter how resourceful these dogs are, they can only get by on their own for so long.

It's a dog eat dog world when resources are scarce.

Hungry and Quarrelsome

Fear and submission look the same.

With no one to care or intervene, rez dogs are free to pursue all their impulses without restriction, including intimidating other dogs. This is especially true when food is scarce. Take a look at the black and tan dog in the center of the photograph, and you'll see the classic signs of submission: low carriage of the tail, an intent watchful gaze with elbows bent, ready to bolt in case of attack.

Actually this poor girl is beyond submission; she fears for her life. Instinctively, she knows she must finish her food before the other dogs (with normally erect tails) finish theirs, as they will invariably turn to her and her food to satisfy their hunger. Feeding hungry rez dogs in packs is not an activity for the faint of heart: enough food must be dispersed over a wide enough area to provide each dog, whether dominant or submissive, a chance to eat without fending off aggression from others.

Like most street dogs, rez dogs have their own caste system...

These dogs have become opportunistic feeders like their ancestors: they will eat as much food as they can while it is available, so they can endure long periods of scarcity. Their position in a pack is never tested as much as when intermittent feeding occurs. Indeed, this is when the true intent and ability of each dog is revealed. One stark reality is obvious, even to the casual observer: there are no old, bold submissive dogs within a hungry pack.

Like most street dogs, rez dogs have their own caste system, which revolves almost exclusively around food and access to it. Sex ranks a close second. Their caste structure is simple and imposed by force: an underdog remains an underdog until starvation, dehydration, exposure or bite wounds take his last breath from his body. When food is the focus, there are no acts of kindness between dogs. If an underdog dares to approach a higher-ranking dog chowing down on a morsel of food, a vicious snarl with fangs bared will be all he gets. *The message is clear: back off or you die.* For the underdog, any move toward the coveted food is a declaration of suicide.

Unfortunately, such bold moves do happen – starving dogs take desperate measures. A typical scenario goes like this: the lucky underdog finds a scrap of food. Higher-ranking dogs strolling nearby take notice. They trot over to have a look. From there it's game over – if he wants to live, the underdog has one choice: to relinquish the food to his aggressors. At times – and for reasons beyond our grasp – the underdog tries to gulp down his scrap of food as fast as he can. Perhaps he's too famished to let go, or to even care what's coming. Whatever the reason, the outcome is the same: the aggressors will attack and kill the underdog to get at his food. And then they'll eat the underdog.

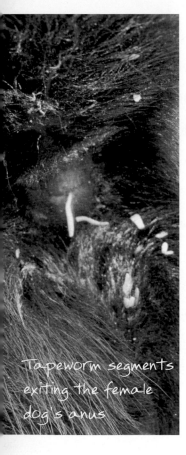

Tapeworm segments
exiting the female
dog's anus

Stowaways

Restraining a dog with no name always carries a certain kind of urgency with it. The worms fleeing the dog's anus have some extraordinary internal compass that invariably points them directly toward the restraining arm of the dogcatcher, which apparently is their magnetic north! The aim is simple: to finish implanting the dog before the parasites make contact with the arm. So far, the dogcatcher comes out a clear winner.

The white flakes tumbling forth from the anus of this dog are tapeworm segments, likely of the *Taenia* species. Squeamish reactions aside, the tapeworm has a rather fascinating and complex lifestyle, starting deep inside the dog's intestine. Often unbelievably long (75 to 500 cm), the worm's body is comprised of many segments, pictured here as white flakes. Within each segment, which functions independently of every other segment, is a reproductive tract loaded with tapeworm eggs. As shown here, these segments, also called *proglottids,* are passed through the anus and dropped randomly into the environment, where an unsuspecting intermediate host (for instance, a rabbit, deer, or cow) unknowingly swallows them while grazing. Safe within the new host's intestines, the young tapeworm hatches from its egg only to make an ingenious breakaway for the liver via the bloodstream. Leaving behind a trail of bloody tracks in the liver, the larval tapeworm drops into the abdominal cavity of its intermediate host. Encysted there, it awaits its next ride toward further development and maturation. When might this occur? Typically, when a hungry dog comes along and attacks, kills, and devours its prey. Presto, the young tapeworm is inadvertently ingested. The tiny invader nestles comfortably into the dog's intestines and, within two months, the hapless host starts shedding tapeworm segments again. So goes the never-ending, eons-old life cycle of this amazingly well-adapted parasite.

Parasites travel on hope. They hope to be ingested by the right host, hope their unlucky host will live long enough for them to reproduce and pass on their progeny to the outside world, and hope their offspring will in turn be picked up by a new host. In developed countries, the idea of humans infected with parasites meets with recoils of horror, whereas in most developing countries this is a simple reality. No wonder people panic at the sight of bloody white worms or ticks clinging to their furry friends: these parasites are perceived as ugly and disgusting, and potentially harmful to their companion animals. Even worse, these unwelcome guests are easily transmitted to doting owners who share their beds and pillows with their pets.

In the wild, parasites are both cautious and ubiquitous: they infect every known mammalian and avian species yet must live in harmony with them. If a parasite infects its host to the point of causing the host's death, then the parasite itself has committed suicide – hardly a winning evolutionary strategy! A parasite needs to feed, and a dead host is useless in fulfilling that basic need. If we subscribe to the premise that there is no "clean" wildlife (i.e., exempt of parasites), then unless livestock is heavily treated with anti-parasitic drugs, the same holds true: there is no clean livestock either. By implication, the rez dog is no different; its body is essentially a vessel for many species of parasites unknowingly ingested whenever the dog eats a prey animal. As long as rez dogs feed off other animals, internal parasites get their meal too (either by sucking blood or ingesting food remnants from their host's digestive tract), and all live happily. The trouble starts for both dog and parasites when the host dog is no longer able to find food. While the dog goes hungry, the parasites continue to feed off its body, weakening the poor creature to the point of exhaustion and death. A dead end for both dog and parasites!

Some say that humans are the earth's greatest – and worst – parasites. Unlike the wormy type, we as a species have not adapted well to our host, the planet.

Somewhere along the way, we seem to have forgotten that our host must remain robust and healthy to sustain our lives. Instead, indiscriminate use of the earth's resources impedes the planet's resilient ability for the balance and harmony that would ensure both its survival and ours. In parasites, we have excellent teachers that have adapted and survived for eons; yet we too fail to learn the urgent lessons. Perhaps, if we looked closely enough, we would see the tapeworms and fleas shrieking and recoiling in horror as they watch humans depleting the earth's riches; and they would no doubt label us a most obliterating and careless parasite.

The Untouchables

For a dog with no name, there is no badge of honour to be an untouchable. He is lonely, goes hungry, and will never fit in. He is an outcast.

She became known
as dishwasher dog!

I'm Invisible

Distrust of outsiders runs deep among rez dogs.
One look at this edgy female tells us all we need
to know: this dog is truly feral. Her fur is dirty
and matted; it's unlikely she's ever worn a collar.
She watches our arrival with a wary eye, keeping
her distance, visibly nervous. There's a good ten
or twelve feet between her and us. As we quietly
approach, she drops her gaze, looks away. Tail
tucked tightly into her abdomen, she moves
further away from us. Food doesn't interest her.
There's not a chance she'll let us touch her.

With nary a struggle or whimper, she submits to whatever might be. In less than a minute, it's all over: her injection is done.

As the dogcatcher edges closer, the skittish animal dodges her and slinks off to hide in a discarded dishwasher; someone dumped it there long ago, with the door wrenched off its hinges. Inside the decrepit appliance, the dog shrinks against the back wall, as though hoping not to be seen, wanting to disappear. As the dogcatcher creeps toward her, she hunkers down even lower, avoiding her gaze until the last possible moment. Then, finally, the dog's eyes – filled with panic – turn to the catcher's, desperately seeking an escape route from her refuge before the catcher makes her own move. Ten feet, eight feet, and then only six feet away, the dogcatcher is closing in. Four feet left… the dog's whole body is tensed and ready for flight, her eyes darting anxiously from side to side. With less than three feet between her and her would-be captor, she makes her bid for freedom, launching herself from the dishwasher in a mighty leap. Much to her astonishment, the dogcatcher reaches out and deftly grabs her in mid-air. With a firm grip, she lowers the frightened animal gently to the ground. The dog goes quiet, no fighting back, no snarling, no biting. With nary a struggle or whimper, she submits to whatever might be. In less than a minute, it's all over: her injection is done.

Carefully, the dogcatcher releases the dog from her grasp. The moment her feet touch the ground, the animal is off like a shot, running flat out to freedom, not once looking back. We stand there watching her go, amazed: so fearful, yet she never once tried to bite any of us. How long will it be before she feels the touch of a caring human hand again?

This aloof, submissive dog is one of many "untouchables" we encounter on First Nations reserves. They're easy to identify: they look and act defeated, avoiding both eye and body contact with others, whether human or canine. Their signature behavior is the full tail tuck under the abdomen. The solitary quest for such a dog? Simply to survive, one day at a time, without injury.

Downtown Dog

Lurking on the fringes of society, homeless dogs are torn between opposing forces: the need for food on one hand, the desire to avoid contact with humans on the other. We encounter this young dog on an excursion to the small town bordering the

For an untouchable, playing safe is not an option. Life is about constant exploration, making mistakes and most of all trying to overcome fear.

reserve. Driving up the main street, we first notice a few dogs wandering in and around the downtown area. As we watch in amazement, someone in a minivan parked outside the legion hands an entire hamburger out the window to a hungry and grateful street dog. What a feast! He gulps it down greedily, in two quick bites.

Doubling back, we head for a park area where we earlier spotted a dog lying in the shade of a dumpster in a back alley. From what we can see, this wily fellow has already been through the garbage and helped himself to whatever tasty remnants he could find. We

quietly approach and manage to coax him away from his safe spot with some treats thrown his way.

But that's as far as we get, he refuses any help from us. How can this guy understand that we're offering him a chance at a better life? His comfort zone is relatively small, and he only lets people approach him if they keep their distance; three or four feet away is as close as we can get. Any attempts to sneak closer and he starts edging away sideways, his wary eyes locked on us the whole time, always maintaining that safe distance. If we accelerate our pace to close the distance, he tucks his tail close to his body, crouches his rear end to the ground, and explodes into a cannonball sprint, darting furtive glances backward to assess the success of his escape strategy, much like a coyote would. No matter what our tactics, we can never get near him. Finally we call it a day and back off; he's still eyeing us suspiciously as we drive away. Unless we can come up with another plan, he'll stay put where he feels safest. The dumpster zone is his home – for now anyway.

"The weak can never forgive. Forgiveness is the attribute of the strong."

– Mahatma Gandhi

Forgiveness

Sometimes even the best intentions go awry – and a hapless creature takes the brunt of the error. When you gaze into her eyes, you can still see the terror she experienced and shared with her captors. The dogcatcher screwed up: her vast medical knowledge had not prepared her for what was about to happen. This female dog lived with four other female dogs: three were her sisters, and the oldest was her mother. Although the owner of the house scattered food on the ground often enough to keep these five related dogs from wandering far, they were still semi-feral dogs, difficult to approach and capture for contraceptive implants.

Young as she was, this female had obviously had several litters already. While we were able to catch three of the other females with offerings of food and help from the young man at the house, none of us could get close enough to grab this elusive dog. It was time for Plan B. Out came the smelly canned food, which we spread around for the pack. As expected, they went for it. All it took was a moment of distraction for the dogcatcher to deftly drop the noose of the rabies pole over the dog's head. Terrified by the sudden pressure on her neck, she began yelping and writhing on the ground, pulling the noose around her neck even tighter. This type of response to restraint was expected, and we reacted accordingly, moving in with thickly gloved hands to gently but firmly hold her still. Once that was achieved, the offer of more smelly canned food would keep her occupied and reward her for calming down as the noose was loosened. In mere minutes, the implanting would be over. Or so we thought.

Reality was much different: what we had *not* anticipated was how quickly her mother and sisters would jump in to viciously attack her. In a flash, the dog's female relatives were baring teeth, lunging at her flanks, ready to tear her apart as the vulnerable animal continued her frenzied yelping and rolling. We reacted with a flurry of kicking feet and vociferous commands of "NO!" that prevented the other dogs from doing our captive any harm. Recognizing that we were now in charge, the aggressors backed off and resumed eating the food scattered on the ground. Relieved, we turned our attention back to our reluctant – and still trembling – patient, holding and comforting her as she received her implant. Then the noose around her neck was removed, and she was set free. She bolted as soon as the dogcatcher's arms released her, streaking away as quickly as her legs would take her, desperate to escape the frightening event that had just unfolded. After a forty-yard sprint, she stopped suddenly and turned back to stare at us, as though trying to process what had just happened. That brief moment is captured in the photograph.

Her trauma was short-lived, much to our relief. We have seen this guarded dog on each of our return visits to the reserve. She is in fine shape and though she's still elusive, she doesn't appear to be harboring any grudges. In fact, she and her familial pack behave as though nothing ever happened.

This female dog, her siblings and her mother are free to roam for miles on end. They are likely living the life of their early ancestors, for which the only boundaries were set by the presence of predators or other territorial canids. But regular meals are a powerful lure for hungry dogs: as long as food is provided to this female pack, even on an intermittent basis, they will come back every night to den under the house.

"If you talk to the animals,
they will talk with you and you
will know each other. If you do
not talk to them, you will not
know them and what you do
not know, you will fear. What
one fears, one destroys."

– Chief Dan George

The Fearful Beast

Some rez dogs take one look at us and hightail it in the opposite direction. But not this fierce male: he comes at us with full force to let us know we are not welcome on his turf. Although there are another five dogs around this house, only two cannot be handled. An older female, unnerved by our approach, flees into the forest and watches our activity from afar, while this bruiser of a dog charges straight at us. But he stops short and never makes contact: he still fears humans enough to maintain a safe distance. An outcast among both dogs and people, the glowering animal has no name and the owner of the house does not want him around. The odds are against him on every count: he's short haired, lacking in congeniality, forced to scavenge for food, and – judging by his pot-bellied appearance – heavily parasitized. His longevity will likely be less than one winter.

Fear is necessary to survival. Without the learned or intuitive apprehension triggered by the anticipation or presence of danger, the longevity of any living being becomes jeopardized. As we are socialized and

Fear is necessary for survival.

conditioned to our environment, we become less fearful: outcomes are more predictable. Both humans and animals tend to respond the same way to fear, by either fighting or fleeing. If we have a chance to escape intact from danger, our genetic memory prompts flight as the best strategy for survival. If trapped, then fighting becomes the natural evolutionary response.

With prolonged exposure to danger, unfortunately, a toxic derivative of fear emerges to override our natural ability to respond appropriately: aggressiveness. The dog pictured here exemplifies this to perfection: his fearful association with humans has sparked his aggressive posturing. Over time, his fear has become ingrained; he is now so fearful of people that he shows overt aggression toward us who wish him no ill will. Worse yet, his aggressive stance – born of fear – in turn creates fear in us. If forced to handle him, we would likely do so more vigorously than with a compliant dog, all the while anticipating his unpredictable hostility and fearing for our own safety. Fear breeds aggression, and aggression often leads to destruction.

How does one dissipate fear? Only by understanding that on the other side of fear is freedom. If this dog manages to lose his fear of humans, he will be able to move freely, as non-feral dogs on the reserve do. The transition takes much time and effort, but creating new human associations for these dogs – that do not engender trepidation or apprehension – is certainly possible. This is the only way to free them from their chains of fear and aggression. Will someone care enough to take on the challenge of reforming this fearsome boy? Or will his time run out before he ever has that chance?

"You may be deceived if you trust too much,
but you will live in torment if you do not trust enough."

– Frank Crane

Homeless

Where do rez dogs come from, and what brings them here? In most cases, their roots remain a mystery. This Husky type dog has claimed the area around an abandoned house as his own. Or perhaps he has always lived here. Sometimes when residents of the reserve uproot and move to another house, they leave their "outside" dogs behind, since many of the animals have never been collared and leashed, or traveled in a vehicle. Watching this Husky cross – healthy enough, but guarded – we can't help but wonder about his origins. On occasion we encounter dogs – like this one – that do not fit the typical rez dog profile. Have they been abandoned here? Possibly. Or perhaps they were once pets of local residents that, when given freedom, decided to make their own way.

These misfit dogs are conspicuous by their less diluted breeding stock; they have not likely evolved on the reserve. We have seen chows, German shepherds, and retrievers out here, but never small-breed dogs.

However, these dogs of respected lineage can only be given a home and a name if they let us touch them and voluntarily jump into our vehicle. Otherwise, their homeless lives will continue. On a few occasions, we have baited the dogs with food and trapped them in cages, with disastrous results. Some promptly turn on us with bared teeth and lunging mouths; others express their extreme fear through profuse defecation and urination. As sad as it is to witness, the heartbreaking reality cannot be denied: for these aloof dogs, the human bond – if it ever existed – has been broken. Can it ever be mended? Possibly, but it will be difficult.

Dogs living on the fringe make the asymmetry of trust painfully obvious: *trust takes a long time to build, and no time at all to destroy.* When we as humans fail in our efforts to establish contact with a dog like this one, who loses the most? Does the dog – for not being able to trust? Or do we – for being judged untrustworthy?

Genetic Brothers

Rez dogs are always on the lookout for a morsel or two. Ever the opportunists, they will eat most garbage and sometimes catch rodents and insects to keep starvation at bay. A light-haired feral dog like this one is an unusual sight here. Although we suspect that some feral dogs might interbreed with coyotes, we can never be sure. This dog, however, has the furtive stance typical of coyotes, the same body shape, and a light-colored coat rarely seen in the feral dogs we observe.

As much as we may surmise about the genetic proximity of dogs to their wild counterparts such as wolves and coyotes, they are in fact a world apart. Science claims that only a 0.2 percent difference exists between dog DNA and wolf DNA, and a 4 percent difference between dog and coyote DNA. While wolves and dogs are almost identical genetically, no one would expect to bring a wolf cub home and tame it like a domesticated dog. The 0.2 percent difference would seriously get in the way. So why do we expect the reverse when we release dogs into the urban or rural landscape and expect them to survive? Is this not the same as taking a young chimpanzee into our home and expecting it to thrive like one of our youngsters? Or, conversely, taking a human into the jungle, dropping him off and expecting him to thrive on his own – instinctively knowing what to eat, how to hunt, and how to defend territory and body? Yet chimps and humans share more than 98 percent of our DNA. Obviously the remaining 2 percent difference manifests itself greatly in the phenotypic expression of our genes: in physical appearance and ability to interact with our environment, we are colossally divergent.

Although wolves and dogs are closely related and share several similarities, their biggest difference arises from the domestication process that occurred over some 15,000 years. Because of it, dogs cannot learn

As much as we may surmise about the genetic proximity of dogs to their wild counterparts such as wolves and coyotes, they are in fact a world apart.

the ways of the wild in only a few generations, just as wolves cannot learn the ways of human societies. Take a look at wolves reproducing in zoos – they retain their feral "edge" as much as dogs living free on the reserve retain some tameness. Neither species is able to adapt enough to survive in the other's environment on short notice.

Wolves have a hierarchal and complex pack structure. Dogs, even when they go feral, have a very simple and malleable pack structure. Wolves relentlessly test dominance among members of a pack; most dogs seem content to accept an established hierarchy without a need to constantly test it. In a wolf pack, only the alphas lift their legs to urinate; the other members tend to squat. For dogs, conversely, lifting of the leg for urination is more gender driven than dominance driven. In a wolf pack, only the alphas are allowed to breed, and they produce one litter per year; the entire pack then helps to feed, protect, and raise the pups. Dogs gone feral, on the other hand, fare badly: all females (not only the alpha ones) are generally bred twice yearly, regardless of seasons. And the mothers alone shoulder the daunting task of raising and feeding their pups, in an endless cycle that repeats over and over.

Physically, wolves are strong animals; they are also clever (they know how to get out of a situation) and wise (they know not to get into the situation in the first place). Dogs are plainly less intelligent and usually not as strong. Wolves are active and able hunters, but dogs have lost the ability to subtly interact and connect with pack members as required for efficient big game hunting. Wolves in motion are beautiful to watch, and they can pace effortlessly over long distances. Dogs trot rather than pace, thus wasting energy. Unlike wolves, dogs display a wide variety of postures and other means of nonverbal communication that reveal their state of mind; this ability is clearly an advantage that supports their survival within human societies.

Thousands of years have gone into the process of domesticating dogs, socializing them to the presence and companionship of humans. When dogs are abandoned or neglected, their domestication, indelibly imprinted in their genetic memory, becomes their biggest obstacle to survival. The grim reality is that most, when left to fend for themselves, do not last long.

After being caught and held for a contraceptive implant, this dog – like many others – was loath to leave the arms of her captor.

Loath to Leave

Among feral and semi-feral dogs, one commonality is apparent: none will readily accept the touch of a human hand. Only with an incentive of some sort will they allow any contact at all. To handle already-socialized companion dogs, we typically use three types of rewards: a gentle touch, such as a head pat or a belly rub; interspaced praises of "good dog," delivered in a soft, cheerful voice; and tasty treats. When handling people-wary rez dogs, however, only the latter – the edible choice – has even the slightest chance of success.

The most surprising fact of all? Once a rez dog has accepted a human's touch, we're still only halfway there. To truly succeed, the interaction must be uneventful on both sides: a "no bite" and "no struggle" experience. And for that to happen, we need to guide the animal through a specific progression of moves – a delicate dance of sorts – to gradually build trust.

Once the dog has allowed a human hand to softly caress the side of its neck and chest, we follow up with a slow full-body embrace, gently sliding an arm around the animal's neck and leaving it draped there; for the dog, this becomes a trance-like moment. For what may be the first time in its life, the dog is physically connected to another being, unencumbered by the usual dominant forces of their world, aggression and reproduction. At that precise moment, being touched by a human is clearly a calming and bonding experience for the dog. Even so, we constantly monitor the level of touch and the dog's response to it. A firm hand is relaxing to the animal, but a too-firm hand becomes oppressive and may trigger aggression. If the touch is too light, it may provoke irritation or worse excite the dog.

If held lovingly and firmly, a dog receiving a contraceptive implant, a microchip, and a rabies vaccine will often remain content in its captor's arms, without flinching or trying to escape. Just how comfortable the dogs become is plain to see after all the procedures are done. When the captor's arms gently release their hold and the captive is free to run away, many a dog makes no move at all, preferring to remain in the comforting nest of a warm human lap.

Forever Feral

Feral cats are as much a part of the reserve landscape as dogs – with one notable difference. Of all domesticated animals, cats are the only ones able to live and thrive in the absence of humans. The predatory drive of these adept solitary nocturnal hunters has survived much genetic manipulation since their introduction to human societies several millenia ago.

The felines shown here have found safe refuge in and around abandoned cars on the reserve, with good access to prime hunting and foraging grounds. To maintain its body weight,

an average-sized cat needs to eat approximately eight mice a day. Survival, however, demands more than finding food; cats need water too. Fortunately, they have evolved from desert ancestors, and require less water to sustain their metabolism than dogs of similar size – a true benefit when living the feral life.

Despite this edge, rez cats are as vulnerable to mortal perils as any animal roaming free. Fights with other prowling cats can leave them with severe scratch and bite wounds. Predators such as dogs (feral or otherwise), coyotes, eagles and owls are a constant threat, and will chase, maim and kill unsuspecting felines. Some cats are struck and killed by motor vehicles; others succumb to infectious diseases. Few cats in the wild live to see old age. Even so, their numbers have not dwindled. As long as there are wild birds and small rodents to eat, feral cats will remain part of the urban and rural landscape. Unfortunately, decimation of local wild bird populations by cats is a concern in some urban areas; as always, balance is key. Unlike cats, feral dogs are not sophisticated hunters, either alone or in packs, and the intense selective pressure imposed by humans in the last century has usurped any hope of that ever becoming a possibility (think Maltese or Great Dane).

Living in the Moment

"There is no cure for birth or death, save to enjoy the interval."

– George Santayana

Life is a Surprise

Many of the rez dogs slink away when they see us approach, but for a few, curiosity wins out. This semi-feral puppy, well socialized by local children, was unique among reserve dogs. She had a desperate need for attention and – as we quickly discovered – was incredibly talented at getting it. She was hell-bent on exploring the world and there was no stopping her. While we tried to attend to the other dogs, this little mischief-maker persisted in nuzzling and pawing, interfering at every turn. Exasperated, we finally grabbed her and put her into an empty trough to contain her for a few minutes

> For this young dog, life was a gift, not a
> punishment – a mystery to be lived, but not
> solved, one breath at a time.

– but she was out again in no time. "Into the Trough" soon became a game, and this puppy was calling the shots to perfection; she obviously enjoyed the thrill of being airlifted into the stainless steel tub. Once there, she would sniff around for a millisecond, as though to orientate herself; then she'd pop her head up with a look that said, "Hey, where's all the attention gone?" With an exaggerated leap, she'd fling herself out of the tub and dash back at warp speed to the centre of all the action. Wherever she saw the attention of human hands was where she wanted to be. As much as we tried, our serious focus on accomplishing our tasks with the other dogs was no match for her lively exuberance.

On a windy, sunny 15ºC day, this energetic puppy was in full play mode, trying to entice anyone with two or four legs to join in the game of life, even as she was receiving an implant. Sadly, when we returned to check on all the dogs four weeks later, this puppy had disappeared.

Life is what the playful puppy in the trough demonstrated so well: it always comes as a surprise. There is no rehearsal for living this life. You cannot prepare, you can never be ready, and you simply cannot imagine what is coming next. Life is like that: you have to live it in the moment, always between the "be" and "becoming," the gap where your whole life is really contained. This puppy, intensely tuned into seizing each challenge as an opportunity for growth,

was a true original, taking risks and accepting life's hurdles without hesitation. Brilliance and intelligence shone through her spontaneity; she had no time to waste imitating anyone else. Taken unaware by our sudden presence, she decided the only way to get on with life was not to lag behind, but to create her own actions in response to ours. She could have withdrawn, but instead she joined in, rejoicing in matching our moves. In doing so, she unknowingly expressed a tremendous affirmation for life. In the few moments we spent with her, we all sensed her ultimate ecstasy in being alive. This puppy *lived* her actions and interactions wholeheartedly and in totality, so utterly absorbed by the present that she had no time and no energy for the past or the future. She bounced from moment to moment with joyful abandon and boundless cheer. She could have been a spectator, watching our actions from afar, but no – she chose to be engaged. For this young dog, life was a gift, not a punishment – a mystery to be lived, but never solved, one breath at a time.

A Life Worth Living

Longevity is a rarity among reserve dogs, but here we have a true survivor. It's hard to imagine how a dog could live so long in these harsh conditions, but residents pegged this dog at sixteen years old. She has an enlarged belly typical of dogs heavily infected with worms, her bony elbows are abducted indicating chronic painful arthritic joints, and her hair coat is sparse. Patches of her skin are leathery black, likely from mite infestation, and she constantly scratches at her flanks with her rear legs. Her sad eyes stare vacantly with the vitreous appearance characteristic of cataracts, and she appears very emaciated. She's obviously given birth many times: her mammary glands are hairless, pendulous and dried up. Her physical appearance reveals her stoic survival for well over a decade of winters, if not indeed sixteen of them. Ever watchful, she keeps her distance from humans, and refuses to allow anyone near enough to touch her. Maybe this is how she has managed to live for so long.

Does this tired old girl have a life worth living? Although some would claim she has lived a full life, others would quickly assume that misery has been her lot. Some people might think it kind to euthanize her before winter comes, while others would strongly assert that preventing a life from following its natural course is blatantly disrespectful. Of course, a person with medical knowledge might answer this question

"I know God will not give me anything I can't handle. I just wish that he didn't trust me so much."

– Mother Teresa

> If one witnesses suffering, but intentionally interprets it as non-suffering so as to not take responsibility for it, one goes against one's own comprehension of reality.

very differently than a Native elder who has lived alongside this dog for years. Because we tend to view the world not as *it* is, but as *we* are, our interpretation of the world is shaped by our experiences, beliefs, and culture, not just by how our senses perceive reality. In effect, our view of the world reflects a self-centered perspective.

What was the answer for this bedraggled creature? The local Native elder and a medical professional discussed her situation, each trying to fill in the gaps of her past, the missing details in the reality of this ancient dog – though these details were obviously limited by each person's understanding of reality. In a case like this, problems arise when either person acts in a way that contradicts the truth of her own interpretation. If one witnesses suffering, but intentionally interprets it as non-suffering so as not to take responsibility for it, one goes against one's own comprehension of reality. If a person does that often enough, their sense of certainty vanishes, while expressions of insensitivity become more deliberate. Such incongruence is a small step on the road to insanity.

In this case, the wish of the Native elder was to leave the dog to live out her fate, and that wish was respected. All that remained was to make her as comfortable as we could. Before leaving, we inserted dewormer tablets into soft food, threw the tempting morsels to the old dog and her pack mates, and left some kibble behind for them. For the next few meals, at least, they would not have to scrounge.

Catch Me If You Can

Even homeless pups – like this watchful fellow – have an inherent urge to play. And what a character this little guy is! When we first meet him, the male puppy appears to be about six months old, full of energy and ready to frolic. Leery of people, he keeps a safe distance between us. Crouching, barking, running back and forth, he constantly seeks our attention, but won't ever come close enough to allow himself to be caught. His behavior tells us he wants to be friends, but he doesn't know how. Or maybe he knows, but just can't trust humans. He lingers nearby, constantly beseeching us for a glance or some food thrown his way. Every time we put food on the ground and back up five paces, he lunges forward to grab a piece or two. As he does, his gaze remains fixed on us, following our movements, never wavering. If we move even a

On the reserve, the difference between individuality
and personality is quite apparent.

step forward, he bolts back into the woods and eyes us warily from his safe perch, reassessing the situation. Now and again, we indulge him in play, crouching and dodging in response to his lively antics. Once he's had enough attention to satisfy him, he settles down, content to supervise our work from his perch. As we leave, we wish him well and leave more food behind for him.

Sometime during the following winter, this pup and four other dogs in the neighborhood mysteriously disappeared. The occupant of the house nearby claimed that a cougar had been sighted and most likely snatched these dogs and others in the surrounding area. Their carcasses were never found, but on subsequent trips we noticed that the dogs in this area had all but vanished. Lives cut short are too often the reality for canines living wild.

On the reserve, the difference between individuality and personality is quite apparent. "Individuality" is the fundamental essence of who we are; this authenticity is not altered by values imposed by others. In this way, feral dogs are true individuals. The polar opposite is "personality," which is a façade, a pretension created to satisfy the expectations of others; personality drives us to conform so that we behave and live according to society's rules. The more we seek the praise and approval of others, the more personality driven we become. Individuality implies freedom, whereas personality implies bondage. Notice that the companion dogs best suited to live intimately with us invariably have great personalities.

There is a tacit understanding between feral dogs and humans: the dogs must learn to display enough personality to be tolerated near human habitation. But ultimately, unable to depend on humans for their survival, these animals must remain individual to their very core.

A Life of Repetition

Out here, dogs learn the important lessons early, or they don't last. This pup's only chance for survival is to be consistent, and to be consistent means she has to be predictable. If she behaves erratically or unpredictably, she will be ostracized by other homeless dogs. If she shows any behaviors toward humans beyond simple submission, she will be reprimanded, neglected, shooed away, or disposed of. If she is consistent, she will be tolerated because she is manageable and easily manipulated. Even if this behavior contradicts her inherent nature, she would do best to live in disharmony with herself rather than disharmony with humans or other dogs. How else can she ensure her survival? Her mother has prepared her by modeling a spectrum of activities and behaviors that she in turn learned from her own mother. If this puppy fails to live the predictable life taught to her, she will – without a doubt – endanger her own survival.

For a reserve dog, to be consistent means to live according to what has been taught – in essence,

according to the past, the only reference point she has. But living this way is to live a life of repetition: there is no room to grow and explore new behaviors and thoughts. Scavenging for food, seeking shelter, and moving without antagonizing other dogs and humans are her daily activities, her sole focus. Every day, within the small area to which she has confined her life, she repeats the same routine.

Like many people, she lives her life in one dimension, in a familiar space filled with consistency and dependability. To be an adventurer, to explore all aspects of life, to experience the world in its totality – these are luxuries that will elude her, as they often elude us, all for the sake of conforming. And so she lives a life of repetition – but her world is safer that way.

Day by Day

For some dogs – like this one – "lay low" is the way to go. Take a closer look at this big male and you'll see the furtive stance and classic fleeting eye contact typical of nameless dogs. You might say a close human encounter is definitely in the realm of the third kind for this dog: he prefers to leave food behind and flee rather than stay and risk being touched. Everything about him smacks of a strong survival instinct: he is not the largest or the most alpha, but he is one of the most resilient dogs around. He knows how to interact with other dogs and is always able to nab a piece of food without eliciting aggression from the dominant few. He interacts with them, but in a satellite manner, always gravitating to the edge of a pack's territory,

He radiates a kind of acceptance of life that
could easily be viewed as pessimism.

never jumping into the middle of the action. He radiates a kind of acceptance of life that could easily be viewed as pessimism. When we fill a treat with deworming pills and toss it to him, he gulps it down immediately – little does he know that fate is working in his favour today.

This dog has one obvious advantage for survival in a cold climate – a woolly coat reminiscent of the Malamute. There stops all resemblance: he avoids fights, he does not vocalize, and he carries his tail low at all times. His gaze tells us that he is focused on the present, nothing else. Tomorrow will take its own course, and when it comes he will be there to face it calmly. And if tomorrow never comes, he is here today, alone. As observers, we can't help but wonder: is this a sort of sadness we're seeing in this wary dog? Or is it simply a deeper peace, an acceptance of life as it is? Only the dog knows for sure, and he's not about to let us close enough to find out.

Play gives
every living
heart an
enthusiasm
for life that is
inimitable.

Time to Play

This lop-eared puppy would make anyone smile. She is barely six months old and can't wait to jump into our arms to be held; the implant process doesn't bother her at all. As far as she's concerned, life is a fun journey of discovery, and she shows no apprehension toward it. Her intent, clearly, is to dive with great gusto into every moment she's granted, and engage anyone with a beating heart to share in the fun. Without knowing it, she emanates a strong and loving energy that embraces everything and everybody. Even through the eye of the camera, there's no mistaking her mischievous intent: she is actively looking for action, bounding about like a little tease, hoping one of us will chase after her and play.

What is most apparent in rez dogs like this playful puppy is the uncanny ability to shut out both the past and the future and fully engage in the present moment. The concept of self-absorption, so inherently human, is totally absent in feral dogs. Once their survival needs are met, most seem to rejoice in life, not for its outcomes or rewards, but simply and purely for its own sake. Their very existence exemplifies a force of nature devoid of mean-spiritedness and unnecessary violence or negativity. In truth, dogs with no names are the paragon of self-actualization. Even in the most wretched circumstances, they routinely deal with the unknown with a sense of acceptance. Unlike humans, they have no need to exert control over others. A strong sense of inner-directedness, coupled with an almost endless enthusiasm for life, carries these homeless animals through their many daily challenges.

All her behaviors signal that life is not only worth living, but worth living well.

Dozing

As the seasons here come and go, so does life ebb and flow. Today the rays of the sun are warming and the dogs are coming out from hiding to enjoy the first spring heat. A light breeze wafts over fields thick with growing grass. Summertime is near and the living is… easier. A pup lucky enough to have survived the winter thanks to the abundant straw bedding is blessed – she can live happily and in the moment. Much less energy is required just to stay alive and there is more time to devote to dozing …

A Second Chance

It is true that once given a name, a dog will
faithfully travel countless miles in its life
to respond to the command 'come'.

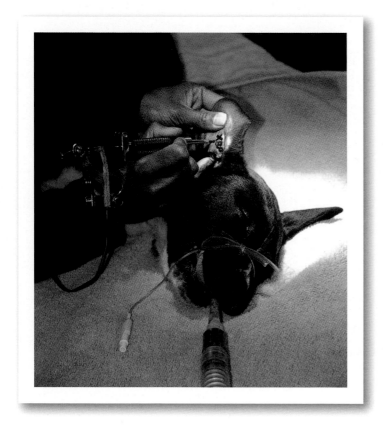

XBP 499

Females aren't the only reserve dogs that need our attention. This male dog, under general anesthesia for castration surgery, is getting a tattoo before his procedure. A mixture of isoflurane gas and oxygen, delivered to his lungs through a tube inserted into his trachea, keeps him unconscious and pain free. His brand new tattoo is XBP 499, and for now that's his only name tag.

When XBP 499 was brought in from the reserve one cold winter's day, he was in rough shape. He still had all of his deciduous or "baby" teeth, which told us he was likely less than four months old. Bone rack thin, this short-haired pit bull cross weighed in at a mere 23 pounds, and was passing numerous eight-inch-long skinny white worms. From what we could see, this pup was going nowhere fast: his life on the rez would likely be counted in days, weeks at the most. He was already fearful of humans, and wary even around other gentle dogs. Whenever someone approached to touch him or pet his head, the terrified pup fled, yipping and yowling as though he'd been gravely hurt. Yet twenty-four hours after leaving the rez – and several hand-fed treats later – he was accepting everyone in sight as his new best friend. How did the taming process happen so fast, when for some it is not possible at all? The reason is simple: because he was so young. Puppies adapt quickly.

And what a transformation! When first retrieved from under a house porch on the reserve, this singleton pup was terrified of people. Each time the dogcatcher's hand reached for him, he backed away, making no move to bite but frantically barking, hoping the threat would go away. Finally cornered, he tried to escape but was quickly "scruffed" and gently held low to the ground. When held firmly, most dogs freeze, while some twist and turn in a desperate effort to wriggle free. This dog did neither – he performed a brilliant imitation of an alligator roll, almost as though some reptilian DNA lurked in his core. And though his jaws snapped wildly and randomly, he (blessedly for us) lacked the coordination to do any harm. Within a day of being in the company of humans, the pup was completely at ease – as most young dogs with no names become. As soon as fearful puppies like this one make positive associations with people, they instinctively want to please us. This pit bull lookalike was no exception, save for the rapidity with which he became a charmer – and a charming companion. When homeless dogs eventually accept people, an implicit deal is made between us and them: for their benefit, the dogs must relinquish their reproductive organs to sterilization, to prevent the birth of more unwanted puppies. They must also receive a tattoo on the inner ear flap, an invaluable aid to bringing pets home if they are ever lost. For now, this puppy is simply XBP 499, but his journey to a better life is well underway: with castration completed, he is off to a foster home to be socialized and to receive a name of his very own. And you can bet he won't look back.

Leo

This little bundle of fur, about three weeks old when first spotted, turned out to be another of the lucky ones. We found him holed up with his mom in a makeshift doghouse in a remote part of the reserve, no littermates in sight. The best option, we decided, was to leave this small puppy with his mother, who was thin but still nursing, until he reached weaning age. In the meantime, we gave his mother a dewormer and left a supply of dog food with the owner of the house to help sustain her body condition and lactation. Though the homeowner cared little about whether the puppy survived at all, she ironically did not want to see the little creature hurt or suffering: in her mind, the responsibility of dealing with the pups fell solely to their mother. Even so, she gratefully agreed to let the puppy go for adoption at seven weeks of age, and also approved contraceptive implantation of the female dog. The pup's new owner named him Leo; how could she have guessed that the offspring of a mid-size black and tan Rottweiler-type mother and a black shepherd-type father would end up with this adorable Yoda face?

Nelson

A wound has healed but a scar
remains... such is the fragility of life.

Ironically, life-threatening injury can be the catalyst that turns
life around for a homeless dog. When this one was brought
in, he was downright scrawny, a shadow of the majestic dog
he used to be. The poor pit bull cross was beyond emaciation,
unable to make even a feeble effort to run away from (project
volunteer) Jack. Not that long ago, this dog was a force to be
reckoned with. For the past two winters, his domain had been
the domestic dump, a much-coveted resource he'd claimed

as his home territory. Rummaging through piles of garbage for food, the fearsome canine bullied other dogs into giving up whatever scraps they found. He ruled the dump and he was ruthless – until the day he picked a fight he couldn't win. Afterwards, his face was a pincushion of pain, pierced with hundreds of porcupine quills. Unable to eat or drink for nearly two weeks, he was defeated and near death by the time we showed up. With nary a growl of protest, the suffering creature let Jack lift him up, his head lolling from side to side in total abjection, worn down by dehydration, starvation and infection.

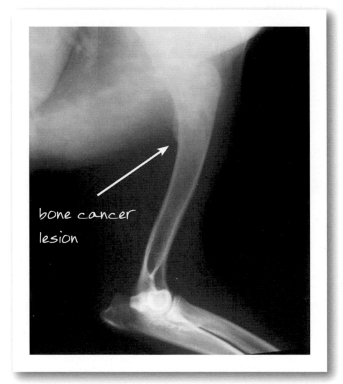

Upon examination, we found that his right eye was partially melted from two quills that had penetrated from the surface of the lateral eyelid. We removed the quills but left the eye, hoping it would heal as the dog gained strength. Within a week, it was obvious the eye was still melting away, getting worse instead of better. And the dog's discomfort was mounting: his front paws frequently swiped at his face, trying desperately to rub his eyes, to rid himself of the pain. With no other choice, we performed an enucleation (surgical removal of the eyeball), with heartening results. He instantly felt better, and it showed: he stopped rubbing his face, perked up and became playful. But even though he was healing, this big dog was hardly an adopter's dream. The strikes against him were many: he was part pit bull, dominant toward other dogs, and black. And if that wasn't bad enough, he was big (sixty-plus pounds), and he was missing an eyeball. Would anyone care enough to take him in, give him a loving home? Miraculously, someone did. Kate and Clay took him home, and they called him Nelson.

But his story doesn't end there. Five years into his life journey, Nelson tests the fragility of life once more. On his daily winter walks through snow-covered mountains, his owners notice that Nelson's right front leg is causing him pain. He shows his discomfort by shortening his stride considerably on his right side.

When his lameness worsens, they know something is seriously wrong. Soon Nelson is lifting his head each time his front leg touches the ground, trying to lessen the weight on the limb: a sure sign of mounting pain.

So Kate and Clay whisk him back to the clinic, where radiographs of Nelson's leg reveal a bone tumour growing on his proximal humerus. And he's hurting: despite strong medication, Nelson moans softly in pain through the night. There's no time to waste – a decision has to be made quickly to stop his suffering. Should Kate and Clay humanely euthanize their companion? Or take a chance and have the leg amputated to relieve his agony, hoping the cancer hasn't yet spread? The stoic dog ultimately makes the choice for them. Despite his grave illness, Nelson has never lost the twinkle in his remaining eye; his will to live is strong. With that, Kate and Clay opt for amputation, nursing their friend through his recovery with love and care, as they did before. Nelson has won yet another reprieve, another chance to live. Now missing a right eye and a right leg, this resilient boy reminds us that life is not always as fragile as it seems.

Date: April 7, 2011	Owner/"Pet": Nelson		Pet ID #: 4869
Pet's Age 11 yrs.	Pet's Weight: 64 lb 29 kg		
Surgeon: Dr. Samson	Assistant: Alex Bogner		

Surgical Procedure: Limb Amputation - Right Front

Pre-Operative Medications:

Sedation:	Atropine: 1.2 ml @ 9:30am Ace 0.06 ml @ 9am / Hydro: 0.3 ml @ 9am	
	BAA: ml @ Other:	
	Dexmed:(IM) ml @ Reversal:(IM) ml	ET #: 10
Induction:	Mask down: [ ] Ket/Val IV: 2 ml Propofol: ml/Ket ml	
	Other:	

Intraoperative Medications:

Ket drip

Cefazolin @ 22mg/kg

Fluid Type: LRS	Volume: 900 mL	Route: IV
Antibiotics: TGH: Cephalexin 500mg 1 1/2 BID x 7d		
Other: Hydro 0.3mL IV TID		

Nelson's pre-op notes

"I can be changed by
what happens to me,
but I refuse to be
reduced by it."

– Maya Angelou

Radar

Radar was another rez dog that came to us in pain and went on to the life he deserved. Rescued from his sorry plight by Jack, this dog came in limping on three legs, not using his right front limb except to knuckle on it at the wrist joint. Radiographs confirmed that his elbow was thickened by a large bone callus: to exhibit that much bone healing, he had probably survived an encounter with a fast-moving car at least two months prior. Unfortunately, his radial nerve appeared to have been irreparably damaged. Two weeks of rest, anti-inflammatory medication and weight support did little except confirm the worst: he still had no pain sensation in his right toes, and his front leg was never going to get any better. His knuckle joint was becoming damaged from being dragged on the ground as he tried to make his "tripod" posture less awkward. Because he was

Imprinted in the genes of every animal must be the famous quote by Winston Churchill: "Never, never, never give up."

suffering from radial nerve paralysis, he was dubbed "Radar," a name that would forever after clue us in to his cause of surrender. We performed a front leg amputation and, a month later, Radar found his forever home with a medically trained person – how perfect is that!

If we look to the phylogenic tree, we see that as animals evolve, so do their nervous systems and their ability to feel pain. To suffer is not the exclusive privilege of humans. Birds and mammals clearly perceive pain and pleasure, although how much amphibians and reptiles do is still unclear.

The way we react to pain and suffering, however, is uniquely "human": the desperation we feel, the emotional devastation we express, and the will to let ourselves weaken physically is not evident in animals. With our four-legged friends, the exact opposite happens: after moments of what appears as anxiety, sadness and hopelessness because of their plight or circumstances, their ancestral genetic memory kicks in and prompts them to move on. Pondering despair and wallowing in misery long enough to endanger their survival never seems to be an option. *Animals always choose to heal, not to suffer*; this cannot be said categorically about humans.

If we study domesticated animals, and in particular dogs – our closest animal friends – for whom the only selective genetic pressure has been imposed by man and not nature, we see that the will to heal still profoundly overpowers the will to suffer and give up. In this aspect, rez dogs have an enormous advantage over most owned dogs, in that they are less exposed to the sensitivity of human guardians. As a result, their strong will to heal still trumps all – which is not always true of dogs that have established too close a bond with humans.

And Radar? Last we heard, he was living the good life and motoring along just fine on three legs.

> "When beset by a physical affliction,
> you can either prepare to heal or to suffer."
>
> – Author Unknown

Red Dog

Nature loves a burst of energy, and Red Dog is just that – and more. Named for her red fur and her bold and confident personality, this sparkly-eyed girl quickly stole our hearts. When found, she was hopping on three legs, her right rear leg held high and dangling. Despite her awkward gait, she was still bright and alert and in constant motion. From what we could see, she had been accustomed to human contact: she showed minimal fear at being handled. In fact, she seemed bent on planting wet, slurpy kisses on every human hand or face that came within reach. A touching gesture, but a health hazard nonetheless

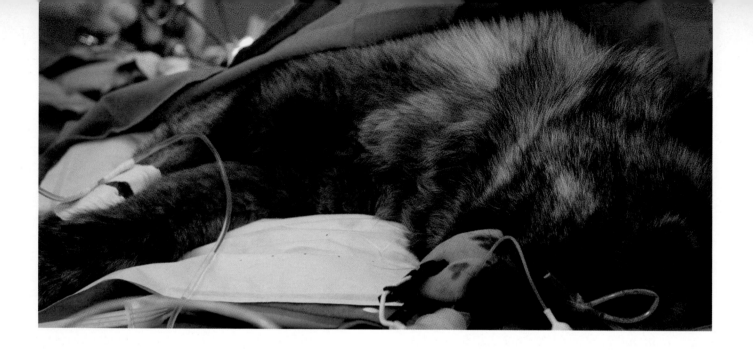

considering the worm load she was carrying from her scavenging lifestyle.

Red Dog wasted little energy on trying to look normal: stumbling was her style. But stumbling is not falling or failing. Dogs lose energy and vitality by being inactive; their strength comes from forward movement. Red Dog knew this instinctively, and was a paragon of vigor and vitality despite her injury. Soon after she was brought to the hospital for treatment, a radiograph confirmed the true extent of the damage. A classic transverse fracture of the tibia had occurred about a week before Red Dog was discovered, judging by the amount of scar tissue formed at the injury site. A vehicular encounter gone wrong was probably the cause – as it is for most non-weight-bearing leg injuries found in rez dogs. To treat her fracture, we inserted a pin in her tibia to heal the bone over a two-month period.

While recovering from surgery, this lively girl was

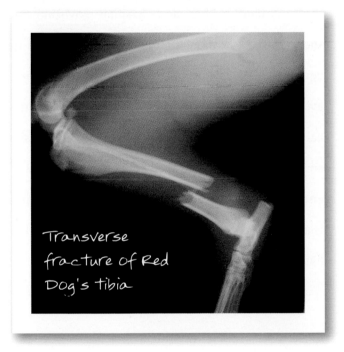

Transverse fracture of Red Dog's tibia

most attuned to her new hospital environment: she explored every nook and cranny, every piece of equipment and, when not under strict supervision, every garbage can she could find. A real "time vampire," she needed constant monitoring, as she simply could not restrain her ever-expanding flow of energy. To come into contact with such a living being is a gift to us all: she reminds us that a meaningful life happens when we are fully engaged.

To receive the blessings of awareness, purpose and courage, we must not only participate in, but also embrace, all new experiences that come from the changes in our lives.

And Red Dog has embraced them all with joyous abandon: this sunny female mended well and is now thriving in the love and care of her new adoptive home.

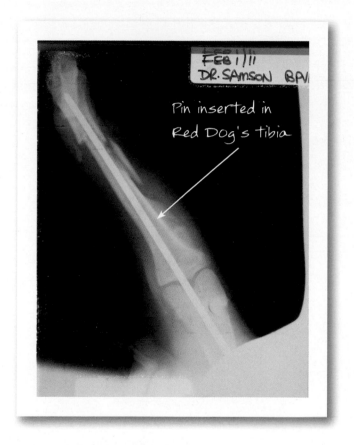

A real rez dog
success story,
Eddie never takes
a single day for
granted. Neither
should we.

Steady Eddie

Sometimes even the most unlikely adoptee wriggles his way into someone's heart. Take Eddie, for example – he was about two years old when he was found wandering the road just outside the reserve boundary. A Good Samaritan passerby picked him up and brought him to our veterinary hospital. As typically thin as most rez dogs but physically unhurt, the timid intact male had no self-esteem and cowered when anyone came near him. He was a black, mid-sized dog, but otherwise unimpressive in the looks department. With his meek demeanor, he attracted little attention from would-be adopters and no one cared to take him home. A month went by, and still no takers. Then, finally, Eddie was welcomed into a family: the dogcatcher's own! Since then, Eddie, with his unwavering pleasant and even-tempered personality, has been both a gift to a family and an asset to a business. He is a testament to the fact that good things come in plain packages. Each morning, without fail, our ever-dependable dog walks the perimeter of the property to mark his forested territory, sniffing the air for the presence of cougars or coyotes. Satisfied, he heralds a new dawn with a long, luxurious body stretch, then heads off to work at the clinic, greeting everyone – animal or human – that comes through its doors.

We could all learn a thing or two from Eddie. Life, in all its glory and adversity, should be celebrated for the pure joy of it, as well as for the challenges it presents that make us who we are. While we should always be grateful for the gifts bestowed upon us, we should remain wary of the pitfalls of complacency, a state of self-satisfaction that keeps us blinded to the troubles and woes around us. If we are content, we have found intrinsic happiness, a state of elation independent of external factors. Contentment is the sense that everything is complete and perfect the way it is. Nothing is missing. It is a most desirable and healthy state of mind.

Since the divide between contentment and complacency is very narrow, how do we avoid inadvertently crossing it? By recognizing that when we are content we live in full harmony with our surroundings, taking

"It's not a big step from contentment to complacency."

– Simone de Beauvoir

adversity and life-enhancing situations with equal balance and sentiment. Contentment is a blissful state to experience, but without any challenge or motivation, we invariably fall into a state of complacency. Animals that have been tamed or domesticated tend to become complacent, as there is no need to move; the will to thrive is replaced by the will to just exist. Rez dogs die if they reach a state of complacency, and that is precisely why previously owned dogs abandoned on reserves to fend for themselves fare so badly. The adversarial forces of hunger and harshness come at these dogs much too suddenly and abruptly for them to deploy adequate coping strategies. What chance do they have? The lesson here is jarring but worthwhile: without challenges to our existence, we can never become what we are meant to be. And once we think we have mastered adversity and move beyond to contentment, the door of complacency swings open and, sadly, we are always compelled to cross its threshold.

Eddie, coming to us from his life of hardship on the reserve, never fails to fully evaluate his world each morning, always content but never complacent. He doesn't take a single day for granted. And neither should we.

"It is a mistake to
try to look too far
ahead.
The chain of
destiny can only be
grasped
one link at a time."

– Winston Churchill

Destiny

Every time a dog is pulled from the reserve, crated like this female, then surgically sterilized to become a dog with a name and a home, we alter its destiny. As we do so, we can't help but wonder: does such a dog recognize that its chances for survival have improved? At the very least, does the rescued animal have an inkling that life is about to get better? Or does the once-feral nomad mourn its loss of freedom?

When monitoring a population of rez dogs, we can quickly see that fate and destiny have favored some and neglected others. And how different their lives are! The lucky dogs are born in the summer when food and water are available, to a mother in relatively good health with a strong maternal instinct, in a sheltered location far from the threat of adversarial animals or humans. But others are born in a snow bank in the dead of winter, to a severely emaciated mother, with cannibalistic dogs nearby waiting to pounce on the vulnerable mother and pups. Although rez dogs appear to have no inner sense of purpose other than to survive, thrive, and reproduce, some accomplish

While fate implies absence of choice, destiny suggests its presence.

these basic functions with little effort while others fail miserably. Is it fate? Or is it destiny?

The words fate and destiny are often used interchangeably but should not be, even though both terms refer to a certain fixed order in the universe. Fate implies that life has been arbitrarily set on an inescapable path, while destiny suggests a predetermination of a certain outcome that remains open to individual intervention. While fate implies absence of choice, destiny suggests its presence. Most of us tend to vacillate between acceptance and rejection of fate and destiny in our lives according to our emotional maturity and spiritual beliefs. When confronted with the absurdity of life, we often welcome fate as a comforting concept: incomprehensible events unfold according to a divine plan for which we are neither accountable nor responsible. On the other hand, we tend to embrace destiny when we believe that even though an invisible hand is at work in our lives, the potential outcome of any event can be shaped – that is, fulfilled or lost – by our response to the event.

Perhaps we can more easily relate to any existence as a seed gently blown by divine breath, and directed to bloom to magnificence wherever it may land. With this analogy, the *destiny of each living being is to use the full force of its energy to flourish in the face of fate and uncontrollable adversity*. In truth, how each life unfolds remains a mystery, since we can only glimpse the effects of destiny and fate one small link at a time. And in the end, perhaps sheer luck determines which living being triumphs and which meets an untimely end.

Whether this sad-eyed dog knows it yet, she has been blessed: fate is on her side today. Her destiny? To become a companion dog to a loving family that will provide her with safe refuge and tend to her every need for the remainder of her life.

Food and Sex, Life and Death

If you are a dog with no name, it is all about food and sex, life and death.

That is the way it is.

Live and Let Die

For some, the credo is "live and let die," for others, "live and let live." The problems that exist on First Nations land are not so different from those on non-reserve rural lands, or even large urban centres across North America. Companion dogs get lost. Sometimes they're abandoned. And they give birth to dogs with no names. Eventually, the local bylaw officer arrives and impounds any strays wandering loose. If not claimed within a short period of time, the dogs will either be adopted or sent to death row. In Alberta, Canada, the city of Calgary, with its population of over one million inhabitants, spends nearly ten million dollars per year to deal with such animals.

Bordering the Calgary city limits on the southwest corner is the Tsuu T'ina First Nations reserve. Vagabond dogs wander freely back and forth across the invisible line that separates the city from reserve land. On the rez side, however, there are no official bylaw officers and no animal shelters. There, a stray dog will roam until mortal perils take its soul to another horizon, or until a kind resident decides to feed him and provide shelter. But how many of these dogs is any person able or willing to help? And how many will they tolerate around their dwelling? Most vagabond dogs want to be near people, but not many people want to be near vagabond dogs.

So how do these surplus unwanted dogs cope? They hang around garbage bins and dumps, scrounging for food. They seek shelter in abandoned dwellings, old sheds and vehicles, anywhere that offers a refuge from danger and the elements. If they don't cause too much trouble, they are tolerated enough that they can live close to human habitation, increasing their chances of survival. Many of these dogs are completely feral: they fear humans and keep their distance. Others, not as wild, meekly beg for human favors. But, friendly or not, tolerated or not, the breeding continues unchecked. Finally, the population of unwanted dogs becomes so overwhelming, the aggravations and dangers they pose so great, that people resort to the only expedient solution: a cull.

Many among us are offended by the "culling" solution. But those taking offense likely know of people off the reserve who routinely shoot "nuisance" animals: coyotes that prey on their dogs, cats or chickens;

noisy crows or predatory magpies that drive out more desirable birds; squirrels that nest in the walls of their houses; or gophers that dig holes and burrow tunnels in their pastures. If we step back and take a realistic look at the dog overpopulation problem on reserves, we do understand why people simply don't want them around. What if the dogs are endangering children, pets or livestock? Or digging and denning under their buildings, to give birth and begin another cycle of misery? How disconcerting and stressful is *that,* with no end in sight? If you were to witness a dog starving, or suffering with disease or injury, would you think it merciful to end its life then? Where would you draw the line?

To live and let die – or to live and let live? The quandary comes down to a moral decision that each individual must make. Granted, our cultural background has immense influence on our decisions – but such choices should not be blindly dictated by culture. Whether the choice is life or death, we must, as sentient human beings, take care to ensure that humaneness always prevails.

"When we say life is
sacred, we usually
mean only human life."

– Peter Singer

Hunger Pains

Where do you find dogs with no names and no addresses? Look inside the dumpsters that line the roads of First Nations land and you will soon find your answer.

Dumpster diving is a daily occupation for feral dogs, and is almost always a solitary endeavor. Once a dog has made the leap and is busy retrieving every tasty piece of garbage within reach, no other dog will dare invade his turf. Once he leaves, however, it's game on. Any other dog tall enough and strong enough to hurdle the bin walls will do so – just to verify that nothing worth salvaging remains.

Despite its rewards, dumpster diving can be a hazardous pursuit for the nimble-footed pros; the bins contain all types of waste, from sharp metal shards and broken glass to chemical substances and rotting organic material. For these prolific scroungers, "stomachs of steel" takes on a whole new meaning.

You might think this agile fellow has it made – he's

one of the few with a free ticket to an "all you can eat" garbage buffet and as many fill-ups as he wants. But the darker reality is this: the scavenging lifestyle is not for every dog.

Indeed, these "fast food" meal deals are available only to the rez dogs that are willing, able, and of suitable size; the very young and the very old are out of luck. Dogs of medium height are best adapted to jumping in and out of dumpsters; for short-legged dogs, the feat is insurmountable. Large feral dogs have no problem leaping in, certainly, but will never find enough food to sustain their body mass – hence

their poor survival overall. Lame dogs will experience pain scaling the dumpster walls, and short-haired dogs will find the chill of these non-insulated metal bins unbearable.

Other challenges? Food intolerance can be deadly for these dumpster divers. So can fierce competition from hungrier dogs that claim the territory around a dumpster as their own. For any dog desperate enough, the only choice then is to risk mortal injury in a battle for food or go hungry; it's a wretched outcome either way.

The Trouble Maker

Like brothers and sisters anywhere, animal siblings on the rez each have their own quirks, their own distinctive personalities. When we first met this floppy-eared puppy and her sister, they were only about five months old, judging by the canine teeth erupting from their upper gums. One was tan with black markings, playful but well behaved. However, her sister, black as night, had already acquired a habit that would get her killed one way or another: she chased cattle. That she would meet an early demise was a given; *how* it would happen was less certain. One day, a cow would get mad and fatally kick her. Or the neighboring cattle rancher, at his wits' end, would shoot her for going after a helpless calf. On First Nations land, fenced yards are rare and dogs are not generally confined; as such, they can be a real threat to livestock. Although neither of these females had names, the homeowner, Mrs. Starlight, was feeding them. She liked having them around well enough – until the cattle chasing started in earnest and aggravated her neighbor to no end.

Thoughtfully, Mrs. Starlight had lured both pups into her horse trailer with treats and shut them in while awaiting our team's arrival. One at a time, these bouncing sisters were held and dewormed, vaccinated, microchipped and, most importantly, implanted with a contraceptive – to prevent the births of more puppies that might learn the life-threatening behavior of chasing livestock. We made a promise to Mrs Starlight: if she could be patient and try to keep the "trouble maker" out of trouble, we would return for the little one as soon as a foster home could be found. In the end, we were able to keep our promise; several weeks later, Little Miss Mischief was retrieved from the rez and effectively "retired" from her exuberant but short-lived outlaw pursuit. Once spayed, she was adopted into a home without livestock nearby to tempt her. Gratitude to Mrs. Starlight and her ranching neighbor for their patience with this cattle-chasing black puppy!

Had this young dog remained on the rez, she would have faced a dismal future. The owner of the house may have stopped feeding her due to her high nuisance factor, hoping she would leave. In the meantime, if the pup managed to avoid being shot by the annoyed neighbor, she would have wandered off to other residences looking for food. She would likely become one of those semi-feral dogs that seek human companionship, or at least tolerate it. Her territory would be somewhere in the narrow space between the truly feral dogs – the ones that fear humans – and humans themselves. And with enough harassment from humans persecuting her for her bad behavior, she would perhaps become truly feral herself.

Now far removed from temptation, this lucky little girl will see her vice turned into a blessing: she'll learn to bond with humans rather than fear them. She'll have a warm bed on cold nights. And she'll get her kicks chasing balls instead of cattle.

"If you don't like something, change it.
If you can't change it, change your attitude."

– Maya Angelou

On the Wild Side

Who knows for sure where any of these dogs come from? These two very hungry edgy canines, though, appeared to be rez born and bred. Identical in age and appearance, they were obviously siblings from the same litter. If not already bred, the female (she's on the left) soon would be, likely by her own brother. Though we knew they were likely too mature and set in their feral ways to catch and rehabilitate for adoption, we hoped to keep the cycle from continuing. But try as we might – and we spent considerable time and effort – we could not lure the wily pair close enough to capture the female for a contraceptive implant.

Feral dogs are as wild as coyotes or wolves, but unlike their wild cousins, feral dogs must remain close to human habitation to scavenge for food, forcing interactions with humans who may object to having such company around. These untamed dogs have adapted to living just far enough away from civilization to avoid people when they can, but not deep enough in the wilderness that survival would be impossible.

Truly feral dogs are almost impossible to capture.

As we've seen, many are able to survive and breed successfully enough to produce offspring as feral as themselves. And that creates its own set of problems. Unlike domesticated dogs that are well attuned to human body language, feral dogs can remain blind to our signals, and for that reason their behavior is unpredictable.

Truly feral dogs are almost impossible to capture.

Even with offerings of food to entice them, they never venture close enough to humans. Instead, they wait for us to depart; only then will they furtively snatch the food and flee. They will not enter a trap cage, even when they are hungry and it is loaded with food. Sadly, even if we are successful in catching a truly feral dog, it may never – unless it is a young pup – be tamed enough to trust humans, or to be trusted by humans in turn. Left to themselves, these feral dogs sometimes form loose packs and become a threat to other dogs, livestock, or even humans. The last-ditch solution so far has been to shoot them, an unpleasant task for the rifleman and, with a less than perfect shot, an inhumane death for the animal. And does this course of action reduce the overall population of feral dogs? Not surprisingly, it does not. How can such desperate measures succeed in the long term, given the dogs' clandestine lifestyle and continued unchecked breeding?

No one likes this problem. And no one seems able to eliminate the problem. So how do we change our attitudes about it?

When a dog decides to share a meal with cats,
many cats become apprehensive!

The Truth About Feral Cats

What do these hungry cats with no names have in common with their canine counterparts on the rez? Here – as on any rural landscape – feral cats compound the problem of overpopulation. Some of us know farmers or ranchers whose barns have been invaded by an influx of unwanted cats. These free-roaming felines seek barns for shelter and the abundance of mice to hunt – certainly a benefit for the farmer who wants to get rid of vermin.

But the benefit is short lived. Inevitably, the time comes when too many cats reproducing means not enough mice to feed them all, provoking territorial fights. Cats are wounded, infectious diseases spread, and anti-social behaviors toward other cats intensify. Unfit cats are pushed to marginal hunting areas, where they continue to reproduce and develop more anti-social behaviors, not only toward other cats, but also toward humans who try to approach them. The progeny of these cats become totally feral.

Who deals with this problem? Many of these cats

are unadoptable: they are afraid of humans, and fear has turned them vicious. So how do we reduce their numbers? And who pays to achieve that goal? Even if we manage to "dispose" of the cats, we know more will flood in to fill the vacant niches. If we decide to trap the cats and have them sterilized – and actually *succeed* – well, we'd need a heart and a pocket full of gold to realistically deal with the problem.

Fortunately, such people do exist. Their caring – and yours – means life for these vulnerable creatures.

Playing Solitaire

This little bundle of fur was born in a makeshift doghouse, without heat, in the dead of the winter, deep on the rez. His semi-feral parents had found a human dwelling where the residents tolerated them, and the dogs had claimed the area as their territory.

This little guy was the only surviving pup of a winter litter. At five weeks of age, he knew no dogs other than his parents – and he'd had no contact at all with humans. Not a great start. If this pup's social isolation were to continue, he would be a poor candidate for

adoption down the road. In fact, his life path had only two possible trajectories: the first as an unwanted feral dog with a very uncertain future, likely to breed his own mother when he reached puberty. In the second – a more promising scenario – he would be placed in a foster home with other puppies before it was too late; learning the necessary doggy social skills would give him an enormous boost toward adoption as a companion dog.

We already had three young puppies, rescued from another location, that were to be placed in a foster home by day's end; fortunately, the warm-hearted foster "mom" welcomed this additional little one into the fold. And what a good decision it turned out to be: the loner pup became "Mr. Congeniality" and was soon the favourite in the group.

Though a bit slow to learn (his mother's milk may have been nutritionally deficient for proper brain development), the puppy's gentle and faithful nature made him a wonderful companion for the foster family that took him in. And they knew a keeper when they saw one: they cherish him to this day.

> "In the pregnancy process, I have come to realize how much of the burden is on the female partner. She's got a construction zone going on in her belly."
>
> – Al Roker

Danger! Construction Zone

To be a bitch with no name can be a deadly fate. And nowhere is that more apparent than out here.

Whether a dog lives on the street or on the rez, the odds of being born female are the same: fifty-fifty. Who gets

This feral dog gave birth to seven puppies the following day.

the pair of ovaries, and who gets the pair of testicles? Flip a coin and take your chances. The bigger question is this: what happens to that ratio when dogs reach three years of age? Anecdotally speaking, among tribes and cultures across the globe, you'll find fewer older female canines with no names than males. But why? Are male dogs just more robust, better equipped to survive the ravages of time? Unequivocally, yes!

A female dog will go into heat in adolescence, usually around five to seven months of age, depending on the amount of available food and her own body condition. She will be pregnant for two months, followed by a two-month lactation period. At the end of her lactation period, she will sexually "rest" for another two to six months before going into heat again. While in heat, she'll be repeatedly bred for approximately one week. Then the pregnancy cycle starts again, depending once more on food accessibility and her body condition.

By the time a female is three years old, she could have produced four litters, totalling an average of thirty puppies. This does not bode well for her. Metabolically and physiologically, puppy production is an expensive enterprise: it saps her energy, drains her reserves. And the process is made worse when she goes at it alone, when food is scarce and when she has to fight for her share. If you are a street dog in India, there is an added challenge: how do you produce live puppies exclusively on a vegetarian food diet? But you must, as there are no scraps of meat to be found on the streets. If you are a rez dog in Canada, prospects are no better. Delivering puppies in the middle of winter – often in a snow depression under a tree – is hell on earth: placentas and puppies freeze within minutes at -20C.

Until methods of non-surgical contraception become widely available, the problem of unwanted dogs – whether street dogs or rez dogs –will persist. On the positive side, people from all over the world are currently collaborating, putting their passion and scientific minds to work to resolve this problem. And that is inspiring. Indeed, there is genius to be found when bright and ardent minds join forces to solve a problem. Only when we give up, turn a blind eye, or remain indifferent does it become a hopeless cause. So persist and continue to have faith: creative solutions are on the horizon. In the meantime, take a minute to drop off some food at an animal shelter. And consider supporting the individuals or groups that devote their energy to tackling this problem in the field. Every bit helps.

These two pups were found exploring their surroundings with four littermates. Their mother was successfully implanted.

Masters of Hope

Despair creeps in when we are plagued by loneliness, and optimism and hope prevail when we are among others: from a human point of view at least, most of us would agree on these as truths. Can the same be said about animals? Do these two little strays moving together for safety feel emotions such as despair and hope? Some say dogs do not experience emotions like we do. Maybe they are right: dogs show their joy in the purest and most contagious way, and their grief in the deepest and most devastating way, both with a degree of honesty that a human can not, or will not, convey. How can we say dogs don't feel emotions when they express themselves through such raw and unfiltered body language as a tail wag, a lowering of the ears, or a curl of the lips? Think about it: we bond with dogs precisely *because* they are capable of showing emotion –

Think about it: we bond with dogs
precisely because they are capable of
showing emotion...

> Dogs, supposedly, have simpler expectations,
> enabling them to accept the present moment with
> no thought of what the future may bring.

and because they do it so eloquently (which is also why we don't bond as strongly with tortoises!).

That hope and despair are the exclusive domain of humans is still a widely held belief. Why? Because both involve looking to the future and anticipating actions or events. As humans, we hope for better times, and sink into despair when we think better times are beyond our reach. Luckily for us, the human brain is able to actively shape the present and the future. Dogs, supposedly, have simpler expectations, enabling them to accept the present moment with no thought of what the future may bring.

Does despair set in only when the inescapable reality of a bad situation can be probed and analyzed? Perhaps dogs are incapable of perceiving this inescapable reality. Is that perhaps why they do not wallow in despair about the present or the future? What we generally see instead is canine capitulation or resignation for the present moment only. Can we say, then, that a homeless, nameless dog just plain feels cold and uncomfortable – miserable even in the dead of winter– but endures the cold while he must, with no thought as to how long that may be? Or is it possible that these stray dogs dream about, and perhaps even hope for, warm summer days – even as they hunker down in the freezing cold of our harsh winters and try to survive another frigid night? And do they also feel despair, knowing that those days of warmth are so far away?

It is hard to imagine that dogs are not masters of hope; a tail ready to wag at a moment's notice seems to be a sure sign that hope is always seated in a dog's heart.

The Will to Live

Inside a crude A-frame shelter pieced together from scraps of plywood, we discovered three puppies huddled close on an old mattress on the frozen ground. Not much protection from the elements on such a cold January day. But it appeared to be an attempt nonetheless, from someone who chose not to be indifferent to the two bitches living and birthing outside in the dead of winter.

This docile puppy was one of the survivors;

several of his littermates were found frozen in the surrounding snow bank. Only weeks old, starving and with a belly full of worms already, he had not shown any normal puppy behavior yet. How could he, when he was barely alive? Lethargic and close to death, the puppy hardly moved. He was too cold, too hungry, too dehydrated to even be fearful of the humans reaching in to grab him, let alone dodge their grasp.

Soon, however, we would see a transformation. After three days of loving care, warmth, food, hydration, and a dose of dewormer on board, this little dog found the will to live. Though he had seemed apathetic, such

... when we insist on being indifferent to suffering, we are acknowledging that other lives are without meaning. And how can that not create conflict within us?

was not the case: he was suffering from a profound inability to respond with any emotion or interest only because he was so physically weak. He did not want to give up, but his rapidly diminishing body functions were draining his life force. Given some much needed medical help, he rallied, eager to participate in life.

Some people confuse apathy with acceptance. The difference, however, is profound: it comes down to knowing what can and what cannot be helped. Apathy is a form of indifference: a complete absence of care or concern. Some will argue that, in difficult and trying times, our indifference may save us from sinking into insanity, that the effort to live "normally" as the world around us suffers unspeakable upheaval actually preserves our mental health. Perhaps. This much is true: when we choose not to be indifferent, we expose ourselves to interruptions in our lives, our work, and our aspirations. Indeed, to be involved in the pain, despair and calamity of others, especially when we have not caused any of it ourselves, can be distressing and troublesome. But when we insist on being indifferent to suffering, we are acknowledging that other lives are without meaning. And how can that not create conflict within us? Our mental health would likely be improved (rather than just preserved) by recognizing some of the suffering, taking some action to alleviate it, and then letting go.

Left to the elements, this precious puppy and his remaining siblings would likely have met the same sad fate as their littermates. He's alive only because someone recognized his plight and valued this tiny being enough to step in. Now that he has his spark back, this pup is well on his way to transforming someone else's life.

... when we insist on being indifferent to suffering, we are acknowledging that other lives are without meaning.

Listening with Intent

Of the seven dogs hanging around a less populated area of the reserve three were found hiding from the rain on the front seat of an abandoned old Cutlass. Only this one on the passenger seat was brave enough to make eye contact and seemingly try to understand the commotion: a dialogue between the owner of a nearby house and our team. It was mid-April, and these homeless dogs were an annoyance to the neighborhood just by their presence. No one would claim them and give them a name. We estimated these dogs to be about 2 years old, a respectable feat possible only when life is played not to win but not to lose. These dogs knew that the only way to survive was to stay down the canine ladder and not challenge dogs or humans.

The dog on the passenger seat, the least fearful of the three, maintained eye contact to figure out our communication gestures and interpret our moves. As you can see, the dog took a keen interest in the conversation, his gaze fixated on us as we talked in the yard. In him, we could plainly see what we already

Look — there are three dogs sheltered on the front seat.

knew: dogs are truly the only companions we have that always listen with the intent to understand and not the intent to respond. The point of the discussion was whether these dogs should be placed in a foster home and rehabilitated to be adopted or left to live their lives of freedom. Needless to say, we were all concerned that any dogs left behind would likely end up with a shortened life, but these dogs being older had already missed out on much needed "social" capital to adapt to a life of companionship with humans. Everyone involved in the conversation seemed to be trying harder to respond than to understand. In so many dialogues that grow into arguments (albeit a civil and compassionate one in this case), our minds

... dogs are truly the only companions we have that always listen with the intent to understand and not the intent to respond.

are generally already made up rather than truly open. In such a "closed" state, we automatically disregard any evidence that contradicts our pre-set conclusions.

In the end, what choice did we have? Knowing that life is the sum of all our choices and these choices impact the lives of others, we hoped we made a rational decision in a world many would consider irrational.

Dogs with no names on reserve land live within a cultural context that we have difficulty comprehending, because we are insulated from it. What is undeniable, however, is that no situation can be transformed until it is accepted as is. And to accept a situation requires much understanding and purposeful listening – without the intent to respond – as so aptly demonstrated by this curious black and tan dog. There are many valuable lessons to learn from our canine friends, and "*listen and learn*" is a huge one.

The Obvious Deception

What you see is all there is unless you look beyond.

Rooting for garbage in
a dumpster

The Dumpster Diver

Here we have a hungry dog and a dumpster… put them together and you'll see some vigorous rooting about for edible garbage. As a passerby, how do you react to a sight like this? With curiosity? (*How did that mutt even get in there?)* With annoyance? (*Another nuisance dog on the loose!)* With sympathy? (*Poor thing… must be starving!)* Or do you simply walk on by, engrossed in your cell phone conversation, oblivious to all else?

Intentional blindness is the wilful ignorance of things or events around us. We use this thought mechanism to detach, to avoid feeling guilty or, at the very least, to prevent any disruption of our own enjoyment of life. We might embrace intentional blindness so we can go on living comfortably without becoming aware. After all, if we are not aware of a situation, how can we fix it, much less feel bad about it? Intentional blindness gives us an "out," a way to rationalize our own lackadaisical attitude toward life.

What we see reflects our thoughts, and these thoughts are an expression of what we *want* to see and how we *wish* to experience the world. We see only what we value. What our mind has judged meaningless or insignificant we cannot see – it simply does not exist for us. Where does it come from, this intentional blindness? Our culture and education initially set the stage, but thoughts are by nature changeable; we must take care not to settle into a state where conclusions become fixed and rigid. If we do, we deny ourselves the freedom to explore, to question, to grow, and ultimately, to find true meaning in our lives. What first came to mind when you saw this animal foraging in the dumpster? Some of us may interpret the dog's behavior as an ingenious ploy to appease hunger.

Others might see it as a desperate act to remain alive. What we see – and more importantly, what we do about it – depends on the extent of our intentional blindness.

Perhaps it's time to take a hard look at ourselves. We all know, for example, that dogs (and cats) with no names are available for adoption through animal shelters and rescue groups. Yet many of us deliberately pay large sums of money to acquire a dog from a pet store. What drives us to do this, knowing that our new pet may have come from a puppy factory, or an indiscriminate backyard breeder, and not a responsible breeder? We've all seen enough media and news reports to know that, by supporting such enterprises, we're perpetuating the problems that go along with such ill-advised adoptions. Could it be that some of us remain unaware of the desperate situation of over-full animal shelters and rescue operations? Or are we practicing intentional blindness?

This hungry stray should not have to dig through garbage to survive; no dog should. But our only hope for change comes through human choices: the more of us that choose to cast off our blinders, the fewer the dogs that will suffer needlessly.

We see only what we value!

What is unusual? A cat and a chain — signs that the animals are being cared for.

> "In any moment of decision,
> the best thing you can do is the right thing,
> the next best thing is the wrong thing,
> and the worst thing you can do is nothing."
>
> – Theodore Roosevelt

Fleeting Happiness?

At first glance, a dog on a chain is a worrisome sight. Most of us assume one of two things: either the owner is neglectful and uncaring, or the dog is aggressive and needs to be restrained. In the case of this furry canine, our assumptions were proved wrong on both counts. Firstly, the owner turned out to be a caring person; she did not want her dog roaming with other rez dogs and getting injured or, worse yet, killed. She'd lost her last dog to this sad fate, and did not want to lose another. Secondly, this foxy little female was very well socialized and showed no signs of aggression whatsoever. The presence of a relaxed cat in the background, well within range of the end of the chain, suggests that this dog is well fed, secure and mature. In other words, this dog is able to suppress its predatory drive to kill any moving feline – or at least this one.

The animal's young owner met us at the door and listened intently as we explained the virtues of the contraceptive program. She was fully aware that, without the implant, she would soon witness scenes from her window that would be unpleasant to say the least. Soon her bitch would come into heat, attracting any number of determined and aggressive male dogs – all with their sexual urges revved into overdrive.

Both owner and pet would face danger if they were to get caught between two or more hormone-fuelled fighting males. Tethered as she was, the female dog would be helpless to escape.

Yes, the young lady was fairly certain that she wanted to have her dog implanted, but her expression revealed that something was still bothering her. "But will it hurt her?" she finally asked. Now the problem with feelings is that, even though they may be honest and from the heart, they can be difficult to articulate. Relieved as we were that this dog was apparently loved and cared for, something still bothered us as we left the residence.

And so we wonder: is life as good as it gets for this little dog? Are the small daily doses of caring human contact enough for her? Can she be happy always on a chain, even with the best of intentions? Or would she be better off taking her chances running free? It all comes down to this: *when* is quality of life better than quantity of life?

To express our feelings may be easy; to explain them is far more challenging. Ironically, this puts us on even footing with our four-legged best friends. This friendly little female stands up and wags her tail when we approach. And again we wonder: is this an expression of joy at human companionship – as is the nature of our best friends? Or is it perhaps an expression of joy at any attention at all, and of hope that the loneliness and boredom will be broken, even for a while?

Under an old abandoned car, the mother checks on her puppies.

> "Think occasionally of the suffering of which you spare yourself the sight."
>
> – Albert Schweitzer

Hide and Seek

Tiny, cuddly puppies. A bashful mom peeking out at visitors. A sweet image, yes? Look more closely, and what you'll see is bleak reality. Just like children hiding under a bed when playing hide and seek, homeless dogs elude people by hiding under derelict vehicles. But they are not doing this for fun; for these vulnerable creatures, it is not a game. They have intuitively learned that this is one of the few places where they are safe from predators. Indeed, the sheltered area beneath the rusting iron hulk is a true haven for dogs, often claimed as valued territory and fiercely guarded.

When giving birth, the females - among the most vulnerable of the strays – search out the sanctuary of the underbellies of old wrecks. Walk by and you'll often hear the soft, muffled cries of hungry puppies filtering up from shallow dens dug into the soft dirt. As soon as we approached, this protective female immediately retreated to her progeny huddled under the old pink sedan. Watching her wriggle into the cramped space, we couldn't help but wonder: how could she find enough room to nurse her puppies without crushing them?

How could we walk away from this? With time and patience – and some strategically placed treats – we coaxed the wary mom out for a much-needed implant. Her sagging mammary glands told us that motherhood had become a full-time occupation over the last few years. While we had the chance, we scooped up the puppies that had survived the worst of winter, bundled them up and delivered them to a foster home. It was only March, after all, and more freezing weather was on its way.

Perhaps for fear of losing our sanity, we prefer not to think of the suffering from which we spare ourselves the sight – like tiny puppies shivering in the cold. Blocking out such heart-breaking images is actually a practical survival strategy, as repeated painful thoughts can desensitize us and ultimately paralyze us into inaction, even depression. With so much suffering everywhere, we all experience the stress and difficulty of judging effectively *which type* of suffering warrants *how much* of our attention. If we dare to focus too long on the misery of the world we live in, mental anguish and emotional fatigue will surely grip us, especially if the source of it is beyond arm's length and seems beyond our control. For the sake of our sanity, we remind ourselves, we should think *only occasionally* of the suffering that we cannot bear to see.

But does deliberate avoidance truly bring us peace?

To avoid the feelings of despair that creep into our consciousness every once in a while, we must do more than turn such thoughts away. We need to know that we are contributing to the welfare of other beings, especially those close to us in heart or distance. A prayer, or a thought on how to make things better, followed by positive and compassionate action, is the only way we can help to alleviate suffering. By now, most of us have learned that indifference is not an efficient coping mechanism. Indeed, turning a blind eye can set off a potent and harmful boomerang: feelings of guilt and sadness for our own intentional inaction or neglect inevitably come back to haunt us.

So, once in a while, when distressing thoughts of the suffering of others cross your mind, take action. *Do something.* Make an effort to alleviate it. Any heartfelt action –whether large or small – will make a difference. And it will make you a happier *and* stronger person.

In foster care, these puppies have a chance at adoption. And their mother, spared the strain of repeated pregnancies, has a chance at life.

So, once in a while, when distressing thoughts of
the suffering of others cross your mind, take action.
Do something.

Dog #64 with
identification field card

203

204

Skinny and Shiny

First, dinner went down. And then it came up. When we spied her, this sleek female had taken cover in an abandoned shed near a couple of houses, miles away from any other habitation. From what we could tell, she was used to seeing humans but was easily spooked and leery of physical contact. She had birthed a litter already and was a prime candidate for the implant program, but despite several tries we were unable to catch her. Dejected, we left a heap of food behind to appease our failure. From her apprehensive gaze, you can see that she was reluctant to eat while we were nearby. Only when we backed away did the ravenous female make her move toward the unexpected feast. Then she wolfed down the food at lightning speed, in desperate gulps as though it would be snatched from her. We just shook our heads: obviously this little girl was not routinely fed. No sooner had the kibble disappeared down her throat than she brought the whole soggy mess back up. Startled by what had gushed from her mouth, she stepped back from the regurgitated food, studied it intently and then peered sideways, as if to say, *who made this mess?* With no answers in sight, she wasted little time gobbling it all up again, every bit as fast as the first time. This time, fortunately, the recycled meal settled where it belonged.

A striking observation about rez dogs is this: they usually have thick, shiny hair coats, despite being lean. How can that be, if they are malnourished? Most feral and semi-feral rez dogs are neither fed regularly nor dewormed; witness their lack of body fat and usual overload of parasitic worms. Contrast them to dogs *with* names *and* homes that are regularly dewormed and fed a nutritionally balanced, commercial dog food. Surprisingly, our companion dogs don't always acquire the lustrous, thick coats that rez dogs do. Worse yet, our pets are often plagued with health problems, especially if we insist on pedigreed pooches. Allergies and infestation by mites are to blame for some of our dogs' skin and coat issues; these can be linked to genetics in our purebreds. Retrievers, for instance, are notorious for both food and inhalant allergies, which translate into skin infections and poor-quality coats. Dobermans, pit bulls, and bulldogs are susceptible to *Demodex* mites that cause baldness, skin irritation, and stunted hair growth. Recovery takes months.

However, if we look beyond poorly genetically manipulated dogs, how is it that rez dogs – feeding on food scraps, dining in garbage bins, perhaps sporadically tasting "real" commercial dog food – still sport an enviable hair coat? Hair coat quality is often suggest some answers. Stray dogs certainly get plenty of exercise and sunshine. They eat less than domestic dogs. Some might argue they eat healthier too: think rodents and insects. They hydrate with untreated, fresh water. And most are sexually active from six

Keep in mind, too, that in this case, natural selective pressure
for short-term survival is strong.

a reflection of what a dog eats. So how can it be that rez dogs – lacking the benefit of a well-balanced diet – have healthier coats than owned and well-cared-for companion dogs? A look at life in the wild might months of age. Realistically, any of these could be contributing factors, but probably the most significant is natural selection. Obviously, dogs with poor hair coat genetics cannot produce offspring hardy enough to survive the cold winter months. Since Darwin's law of "survival of the fittest" often prevails when nature is left undisturbed, perhaps a genetically programmed "healthy hair coat" has become a necessary adaptation, providing these dogs the extra protection to survive the elements. Keep in mind, too, that in this case, natural selective pressure for short-term survival is strong. Shiny coat or not, rez dogs do not live long: their lifetimes are often counted in months or limited years. Should the pups manage to survive birth in the winter, the effects of malnutrition – either in utero or during lactation – can have serious health repercussions, from underdeveloped organs to "runt syndrome." Those hardy – and sometimes just plain lucky – dogs that thrive on the rez have somehow adapted beautifully to their short-term lives.

With nature blessedly on her side, the timid she-dog with the shiny coat has made it this far. We can only hope she will make it to our next visit – and then we will try again to give her a much needed break from the birthing cycle.

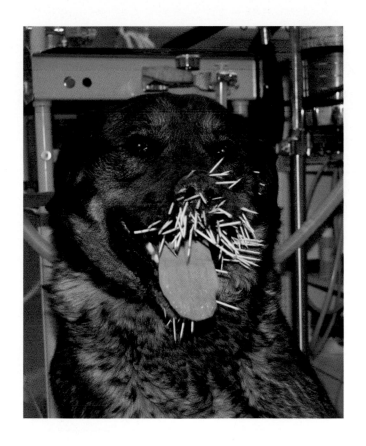

If It Looks Bad, It Is

This forlorn fellow is wallowing in misery, for good reason. He went looking for dinner, and what did he get instead? A frightening barrage of needle barbs. Instant agony. And no dinner.

To a hungry dog with no name, any small creature is fair game as a food source. Porcupines appear to be an easy meal, with their slow and clumsy gait – but as this afflicted dog learned the hard way, they never are. For a feral dog with no guardian to tend to his injuries, the quills deeply embedded around his mouth make eating and drinking painful and difficult. Trying desperately to ease his discomfort, the dog instinctively rubs his face, breaking off some quills, driving others even further into his body. Unless help intervenes, the animal will spend his remaining days in misery; he will likely die of starvation or dehydration even before a mortal infection from the quills ravages his weakened system.

On the day of his rescue, though, this dog is not yet deathly ill. But he is – fortunately for him – much too sore to put up a fight. The tough guy that so defiantly resisted capture in bygone days is now much easier to catch – all he needs is a Good Samaritan to cross his path. Our friend Jack is that and more, spending much of his time and money feeding and rescuing stray dogs on the local reserve. For a semi-feral dog like this, what appears to be his greatest misfortune turns out to be his luckiest break. Found by the right person at the right time, he is spared a cruel, agonizing death. With the quills removed and his flesh healed, the lucky boy is ready for his big break: he is tame enough to be given a name *and* a home.

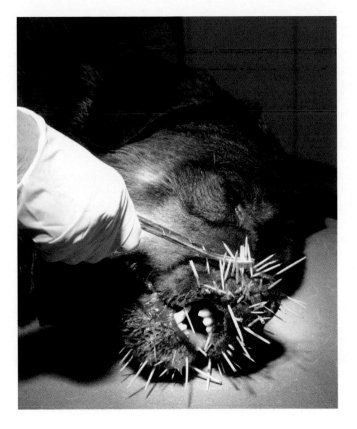

under heavy sedation,
the quills are removed.

If It Sounds Bad… Is It Really?

Feral dogs are wary and suspicious of humans, but most have not fully relinquished their bond with us. For that reason, they are largely unpredictable. When caught, some feral dogs become very passive, perhaps out of utter fear. Others turn into frantic Tasmanian devils. And we need to be prepared for either reaction. Even so, working with these animals brings us two unanticipated benefits.

First, we learn to be present in the moment – an essential skill in the field where a fleeting second of absentmindedness is enough for a terrified dog to clamp his jaws down on whatever human body part is near. Even if we manage to avoid a bite wound, that momentary lapse can mean the hasty escape of a dog that took hours of effort to capture. When we are fully focused in the "now," the needless and annoying constant mind chatter comes to a welcome halt. And we're left with only a feeling of peace and fulfillment, in the stillness and quiet of "just being" that is so soothing to the soul.

The second benefit of our fieldwork is the freedom to express our thoughts as they are, without apology. We say

He is somewhat differently abled, likely from a vehicular encounter while exploring alternative destinations. (He's crippled – probably got run over while he was out wandering.)

it like it is, and no one on our team is ever offended: we all know that our work is done from the heart, not the mind. We vent when emotions run high, and let off steam when it helps to get us through the tough cases. Our passion for the work, and for these animals, comes out in words raw and unrehearsed, with no malice intended. Just as feral and semi-feral dogs wander freely and often without apparent intent, our conversations about them flow freely and without malice.

And if political correctness were a concern? Well, our interactions would no doubt be somewhat more constrained! Listen in as we offer some "translated" excerpts of a typical conversation:

"This unkempt canine appears to have been residentially flexible for some time." *(Looks like this scruffy fellow's been homeless for a while.)*

"Perhaps his owner is too economically challenged to feed him, or he became locationally disadvantaged." *(Perhaps his owner's too poor to feed him, or maybe he got himself lost.)*

"Surprisingly, he appears to be rather chronologically gifted for a free-roaming non-human quadruped associate." *(Seems awfully old for a rez dog on the loose.)*

"Even though he is attractively impaired and somewhat

charismatically impeded, he has apparently succeeded in getting many non-human female quadrupeds parasitically oppressed, judging by the number of offspring in the area." *(Even with that homely mug and zero personality, he's obviously gotten plenty of bitches pregnant, judging by the number of pups in the area.)*

"The non-discretionary fragrance he emanates competes with the intestinal release of his ecologically incorrect expressions." *(Get a whiff of that stench he gives off... and his farts are even worse.)*

"He is somewhat differently abled, likely from a vehicular encounter while exploring alternative destinations." *(He's crippled – probably got run over while he was out wandering.)*

As you can imagine, there's little time to waste on niceties in a fast-paced, urgent, and ever-changing work environment. And while we're on the subject of politically correct language, here is another word to consider: euthanasia. Euthanasia refers to the practice of ending a life in a manner that relieves pain and suffering; it is an act of mercy to end the misery of a sick or injured animal that is unable to recover. No matter what we call it, euthanasia *(killing)* should never be the preferred solution *(first choice)* for management *(population control)* of strays *(unwanted, healthy, adoptable dogs)*.

On the rez, we leave behind all the social constructivism that has shaped our intellectual landscape in the last few decades. The dogs care little about what we say or how we say it. Remember, if the emperor looks naked, then the emperor *is* naked. If a dog looks like he is suffering, he *is* suffering – and that's what matters. Practice compassion: help with whatever resources you have. And along with purpose, have hope and faith – others *will* help with the resources you don't have.

Looking Within

This cheerful dog's most distinctive feature was her incredibly piercing eyes. When we approached, she watched us as carefully as we watched her. Here was a rarity among the rez dogs: a self-assured animal

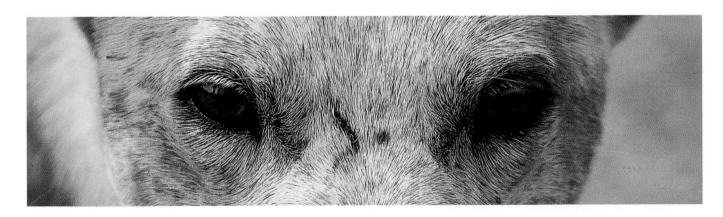

"If a dog will not come to you after having looked you in the face,
you should go home and examine your conscience."

– Woodrow Wilson

with a balanced personality. She showed no traits of dominance, nor of submission. We offered food, which she graciously accepted. We offered some ear scratching, which was fine with her too. Then we came to the implant procedure – which for some dogs will trigger a vigorous protest. Again, our new friend had no objections: she lay placidly in our arms through the entire process. When we let her go, she ambled a few feet away, then turned and stared at us for an endless instant... as though time were suspended. It seemed, in that frozen moment, that this gentle creature could see right through us, as though she could somehow touch the deepest confines of our souls, the hidden parts that even we could not reach within ourselves.

Simply put, conscience is our sense that distinguishes right from wrong. If everyone followed the Buddhist scriptures that prescribe unselfish love for all living beings, then concepts of right and wrong would be the same for all – and free of religious, secular or scientific influences. But such is not the case. It appears that our genetic history, our culture, and our spiritual beliefs leave an imprint on our internal compass, our conscience. When our thoughts and actions are aligned with our conscience, we live with a true and tranquil heart. When they are misaligned, our lives are filled with remorse and guilt. These uneasy feelings linger until we reassess our thoughts and actions and live in harmony with our conscience.

The emergence of conscience is essential to the cohesion of societies: if our external expressions of aggression and destruction are not suppressed, communal living becomes unsustainable. However, the internal compass that guides members of different societies may not register the same readings of right and wrong, thereby giving rise to conflict between people of different cultures. As well, a clear conscience may be relative in time and in the heart it inhabits since awareness of moral values is not standard among all people of all ages. A child may think it

Seeking the best for others through compassion and benevolence does not always triumph over self-love, unfortunately.

fun to harass an animal, then shrug it off and sleep without remorse. An adult, who may have done the same thing as a child, now sees this harassment as improper and experiences moral distress if he takes no action to stop the torment. And since our conscience can be likened to an inner court where our feelings and thoughts battle each another for supremacy, it needs training and practice to become effective. Can it fail us, or default to an easy "out"? Of course it can, especially when the chips are down and the pressure is on. Then we may *purposefully* disregard the voice of our conscience and choose to justify a moral decision based solely on self-preservation. Unfortunately,

seeking the best for others through compassion and benevolence does not always triumph over selfishness.

So if a dog, after looking deep into your eyes, does not come willingly to you, should you examine your conscience? Perhaps! Dogs may not be able to distinguish between moral disintegration and peaceful serenity in a human's mind, but they are extremely adept at reading our body language. In our hectic lives that overflow with the superfluous, we've forgotten the simple body language that exposes our true feelings. But dogs, thanks to thousands of years in our company, definitely have not: their well-being and survival depend on their ability to "read" us. So if a dog gazes through you and into the depths of your soul, remember that he may not be reading your internal compass, but your sensory signals will tell him immediately whether you are in alignment or not. And what did this calm, all-knowing female dog see when she gazed into our eyes and beyond? If only we knew…

A "rottie" is a rottweiler as a "pity" is a pit bull, and muzzling this pit bull was a pity!

A Sweet Pity

Imagine living outdoors in our brutal winters – with nothing between you and the icy chill but a light coat. Could you survive? For pit bulls, or any shorthaired breeds left to fend for themselves, winter can spell doom. Without an insulating hair coat, few will survive long unless they have ready access to the heated indoors. Fortunately, this doe-eyed female has a house address, her own bed in the living room and, of course, a name. No sooner had we stepped out of our vans than we heard a blast of shots fired in the distance. Within moments,

"Pity" and two other frightened dogs barreled by us, straight into the house through the open front door. By the time we reached the door, the well-meaning occupant, who had somehow tuned out the sound of gunshots, was urging them to go back outside and play. Reluctantly the animals crept back out but lingered on the porch, as close to safety as they could manage.

The owner, keen on preventing another unplanned litter, asked if her dog could be implanted with a contraceptive. Thrilled with her preemptive request (how often is it this easy?), we wholeheartedly agreed and set up to do our work. We shamelessly profiled Pity; she was one of the very few dogs that we adorned with a "party hat" (muzzle). Not because she had shown any aggression, mind you – only because of her breed. Bite wounds from strong-jawed dogs really hurt, and they really hurt for a really long time. So we played it "better safe than sorry" and slid the muzzle over her snout, restraining her long enough to implant a contraceptive and microchip, take a blood sample and, finally, inject a rabies vaccine.

Needless to say, breed-specific stereotypes are frequently off base, as this sweet girl reminded us that day. Pity proved to be the gentlest of dogs, bravely submitting to all needles, unfailingly patient with us even though she was to give birth two days later – and ultimately making us feel terribly guilty for ever doubting her at all!

About Carly

Heelers are another breed with a reputation that precedes them. Meet Carly, a red heeler-type dog that has produced several litters already. When we met her, she was in heat yet again, and a throng of would-be suitors lingered around the house, awaiting their chance to breed her. For Carly's owner, a beautiful thirty-something woman wearing the most coveted and fashionable black leather gladiator sandals, the invasion of so many intact male dogs was a major nuisance. When we went looking for Carly, we found her in the hedgerow, entangled in the throes of intimacy with a black mid-sized feral dog. Since any attempt to break up the coupling bond could cause pain to either dog, we left them be. Once the breeding act was finished, Carly happily trotted over to see us, while her skulking paramour beat a hasty retreat into the bush, clearly afraid of humans. Although we could see that Carly was tame, her owner had warned us that she might bite when handled by strangers. We heeded the warning, used a muzzle to be safe, and implanted Carly without incident.

Weeks later, we spotted Carly in the Community Services parking lot on the reserve, but at first did not recognize her as the same dog. She was wandering around the parked vehicles, randomly attacking any dog she encountered. Fortunately for them, all her targets submissively rolled onto their backs when assaulted, thus avoiding injury. Once satisfied with her display of dominance, Carly would calmly walk away, in search of her next victim. Thinking she might be a good implant candidate – if we could just find her owner – we lured her away from her bullying activities. Only when a woman approached us – wearing the same gorgeous gladiator sandals we had all so admired and envied earlier – did we recognize Carly as the easygoing dog we'd implanted

Prejudicial attitudes are pervasive even in the most open-minded among us, despite our best intentions to prevent them.

two months prior. In town, our Carly was clearly not the same dog: she'd become her evil-twin alter ego, growling, snapping and lunging at any canine careless enough to let her close. Her owner promptly ordered her back into the truck, putting an abrupt end to Carly's misbehaviour. Ears back, the dog jumped into the back seat, then turned and glowered, as though we were the cause of her grief. Notably, Carly showed no mammary gland development, and her belly was not enlarged. Assuming a typical gestation period of

about 63 days, the breeding we had witnessed had apparently been unsuccessful. Whew.

Prejudicial attitudes are pervasive even in the most open-minded among us, despite our best intentions to prevent them. First Nations people generally view dogs on the loose as nuisance dogs, as they harass cattle and horses, and on occasion attack people, usually children. If we rely on dog bite studies in urban settings, we might subscribe to the obvious prejudice that male dogs are primarily to blame. Not so on reserve land. Both male and female dogs will gather in "easy picking" areas where food scraps are plentiful – such as dumpsters, or households that routinely feed their own dogs. If, at any time, an inadvertent signal triggers the predator/prey drive, look out. It doesn't take much to set off a deadly attack: a dog gets hurt and starts yelping, for example. Or a racing child, shrieking in glee, happens to stumble and fall. Or a calf, separated from its mother, begins anxiously lowing for her. When triggered, any unrestrained dog with an easily activated predator instinct is liable to join the chase, and sometimes even the attack. On the reserve, female dogs are as likely as males to turn on the unlucky victim; they certainly don't stand back and consciously decide against participating in a pursuit. Witness Carly's overt, unprovoked aggression in the parking lot. Although all of her edgy ferocity was directed toward other dogs, she could easily – in the right circumstances – turn on a helpless child.

In urban settings, dog-to-dog aggression has numerous causes, from poor early socialization to genetic predisposition. Akitas, for example, are by nature socially dominant dogs. Dog-to-human aggression is another matter altogether. On reserve lands, dog attacks on humans are often reported to be perpetrated by dogs with no names. In urban settings, conversely, most injuries are inflicted by dogs *with* names (i.e., known and owned family dogs), and reports point to male dogs as the usual culprits. Rarely – thanks to our government-subsidized animal services and pound facilities – do we have enough loose dogs on North American city streets to form roaming packs, thereby curtailing any consequent attacks from vagabond dog gangs. On reserves, animal services and pound facilities are typically absent. If we rely on urban studies of dog biting, we might easily become prejudiced toward male dogs and their high nuisance factor. Woefully, such categorical thinking fosters a distortion of perceptions. On the one hand, we might minimize differences within groups, condemning them all in one fell swoop: *all male dogs with no names and no homes are a nuisance,* Or we might maximize the distinctions, thus turning a blind eye to potential risk: *female dogs, with or without names, would never attack and maim young children.*

Prejudices – those preconceptions or judgments we form without verifying facts – erect a formidable obstacle to solving problems. Often based on erroneous information, these flawed judgments mold our actions and behaviours. Where prejudice exists, stereotypes – generalizations resistant to change – are seldom far behind. Notably, prejudices and the stereotypes they create grow from a group process: a socially oriented group of like-minded people aim their distorted beliefs toward another group of people – or animals in this case. The target is usually a category of people or animals, rather than isolated individuals within the category. "All stray pit bulls are aggressive" is a typical stereotype. An individual's specific characteristics matter not at all, only that he belongs to a certain group: *this* pit bull may be gentle, but is stereotyped as potentially aggressive (See Pity's story).

Prejudices, we're told, are most often evident in individuals or segments of society with a narrow, inflexible set of social attitudes – those whose world is generally black and white. Since so many prejudices are acquired during childhood, they can easily permeate our way of thinking. Where acceptance of authority is normal and even desirable, children from a young age absorb the stereotypes prevalent in their society. We learn what we are taught. Most stereotypes learned early are never tested; where would we have the opportunity or inclination to do so? We grow up to accept them as facts and truths, therefore unchallenged stereotypes are not likely to change. This early adoption of stereotypes often leads to automatic, effortless behavioral responses. Stereotypes adopted later in life, when we are fully capable of shaping our own belief system through heightened awareness and engaged discussions, are less ingrained and more readily available for evaluation. We all know people who declare themselves free of prejudices; they're likely referring to the ones learned later in life, those they have actively worked at suppressing or annihilating. Knee-jerk first responses, made before we have a chance to think an issue through, are often a lingering effect of early prejudicial learning. These hard-wired, deep-rooted stigmas are, sadly, far more difficult to de-program in our brains.

On the reserve, there exists a different way of living that non-natives may find difficult to appreciate or value – and vice versa. Solving problems on either side of the reserve line will never happen unless we can eliminate our prejudices, or at least suspend them while gathering information. Let's face reality: female dogs *can* – and *do* – attack and injure livestock and humans. And pit bull dogs *can,* without a doubt, be sweet, gentle creatures.

Like a Mirror

These two friendly pups trailed us through the woods on one of our visits to the reserve. What were they after? We were strangers, after all. We weren't offering treats. We weren't even paying any attention to them. But there they were, happy just to tag along – wherever we were going, whatever we were doing. And then we could not help it, we started to play with them and feed them.

Dogs are among the few animal species that have the ability, and the desire, to mirror our behaviours. And they do it splendidly. The secret to their success? Their talent for living at our speed – and responding instantly to our actions. No wonder they're able to fulfill the role of man's best friend so well! Physiologically, their basic body parameters parallel ours in an equivalent body size ratio: their temperature is around 38-39C, their heart rate between 80 beats per minute for large dogs and 120 for small ones, and their breathing rate approximately 24-28 breaths per minute. And with four legs instead of two, they keep perfect pace with us whether we're walking, running, biking, skiing or swimming.

Mentally, too, dogs have learned to adapt to our speed. Unlike cats, which are primarily nocturnal and more independent, dogs have grown to share our daily life patterns – and even anticipate our routines – with the precision of a clock. Our canine pets know exactly when we get home from work or school, the right moment to remind us to fill their food bowl, the perfect time to beg for that special treat. They know, with uncanny accuracy, the exact instant to retrieve their leash for a walk. On top of that, they are capable of learning much of our language, even as they attempt to teach us their own!

Ideally, to adapt to life at our speed, dogs should be introduced to humans as puppies, with plenty of early developmental social interaction to help them cross the species line. From what we have observed in semi-feral dogs, however, even limited human contact seems to achieve and maintain this ability. These two dogs moved with us in perfect synchrony as we walked through the woods to check on a female with a litter of pups. Did they know instinctively where we were heading? Probably. They stopped when we did, waited patiently as we did our work, fell into step when we resumed walking. These semi-feral dogs were not only living at our speed, they were capable of mirroring and even anticipating our actions, despite lacking any experience as companion dogs.

As semi-feral rez pups, these hardy outdoor creatures will likely live a shorter life than their pampered urban cousins. But like all dogs, domesticated or not, they exist within a timeline unique to their species, and to their specific breed: their journey from birth to death is 20 years at best, often less. While we meander through just one of our life stages (childhood, adulthood, or old age), our companion dogs have already hurtled through all of theirs. Unfortunately for us, dogs don't mirror us in one big way: length of life. With few exceptions, we are destined to outlive our cherished animal companions, a reality that brings us much grief and heartache.

While we meander through just one of our life stages (childhood, adulthood, or old age), our companion dogs have already hurtled through all of theirs.

Honouring the Agreement

"You are responsible forever for those you have tamed."

– Antoine de Saint-Exupery

The Social Contract

Among animal lovers, the inextricable connection between humans and dogs is hardly given a second thought. But how did this profound bond develop? Our contract with canines began somewhere around fifteen thousand years ago, when mankind unknowingly started the process of domesticating these extraordinary creatures. The first loose ties were probably established when humans and wild *canids* crossed paths in the wilderness, one a hunter, the other a scavenger. We can speculate that wolves learned the benefits of being in the vicinity of these bipeds and their hunting grounds, scrounging a meal for themselves from scraps left behind. Before long, they were lurking on the fringes of more permanent encampments, seeking any remnants of protein tossed aside as waste by humans. According to theory, wolves with a lesser flight threshold were rewarded with food just by lingering within a reasonable distance of human settlements. One generation after another, their offspring learned the same behaviours. Over time, and initially with mild selective pressure, these animals began severing bonds with their wild counterparts to establish connections with human "packs."

Man reaped the benefits of this arrangement as well: a cleaner camp, free of discarded scraps, and perhaps protection from invading vermin, as well as larger predators. These ancestors of today's dogs likely alerted the residents to any trespassers, whether friend or foe, human or animal. Attachments between humans and canids probably grew more individualistic, therefore more personal and rooted in emotion. It isn't hard to imagine that orphaned or easily

tamed cubs may have been brought into human dwellings as the first "pets."

As these human-animal relationships intensified, they led to increased levels of interdependence between species, and eventually the reorganization of *canids* into forms and functions that aligned with human interests. During the process of domestication, animals under the continuous care of human "creators" adapted by altering their basic nature to meet the needs of mankind. In the case of dogs, probably the most fundamental evolution was their growing ability to read and understand man's signals, even as they lost some of their abilities and their desire to commune with members of their own species. Hence they became loyal to humans, who were now their "alpha" leaders and also their keepers. Over time, the dogs became less efficient at hunting in hierarchical packs. Worse yet, they lost their impetus to limit breeding according to status and, more importantly, according to nature's seasons. This meant that pups could be born at any time of year – to any and every bitch – and whelping females could expect none of the crucial support from their canine pack to rear and feed their young.

From *Canis lupus* to *Canis lupus familiaris*. Did the transition take thousands of years or only a few generations? This question is hotly debated among scientists, but we do know one truth for certain: at some point, dogs developed into their own subspecies – one dependent upon humans. And there would be no turning back.

"Dogs have given us their absolute all... they serve us in return for scraps. It is without a doubt the best deal man has ever made."

– Roger Caras

Cosmic Conspiracies and Celestial Blessings

Take a look at this puppy, she does not have a name but she has a place to call home on an old mattress beneath a truck canopy. She is resting while her four littermates are playing nearby. She is content in the moment. And why not? Chances are this floppy-eared dog has little to fear – but what if she lived in China? Anywhere in the world that we observe dogs, we also see that humanity is not always in the eye of the beholder, and survival is often a matter of luck. While we accept that the status and welfare of animals within any given human society has some variation, such norms are usually grounded within ancient cultural habits and religious beliefs. And these can be difficult to dismantle – even in modern times.

"If you have men who will exclude any of God's creatures from the shelter of compassion and pity, you will have men who will deal likewise with their fellow man."

– St. Francis of Assisi

For a dog born into Buddhist society, the stars would have blessedly aligned, since living in harmony with nature and causing no harm to living beings are fundamental beliefs of Buddhist tradition. Generally, Buddhists choose to live a vegetarian way of life based on the precept of expressing loving kindness. As such, Buddhists see the universe as a totality, with an intrinsic right to exist without threat of destruction from human or divine authority. Crude handling of nature and its inhabitants goes against the acknowledgement that all living beings suffer, and that our suffering links us collectively. Compassion, the sentiment at the very root of Buddhism, promotes the desire for happiness of all other living beings; as compassionate beings, we are "moved" by suffering.

At the other end of the spectrum we find ancient Christianity, whose many adepts took the "dominion over nature" precept perhaps too literally. Historically, Christian thinkers believed that human beings were greatly superior to animals, and downplayed our moral obligations towards them. Their traditional theology was based on three principles; the first declared that God created animals for the use of human beings, so humans were entitled to "use" them in any way they chose. The second deemed animals inferior to humans (citing the lack of both a soul and the ability to reason), so animal welfare warranted no consideration. And the third principle promoted a strong humanocentric (human supremacy) perspective: an animal's value was considered only in relation to humans and not for its own intrinsic value.

Fortunately for dogs, we have seen a significant shift in the Christian perspective. The modern view rejects the inhumane treatment of any animal capable of displaying sufficient consciousness and self-awareness as ethically and morally wrong, and upholds an animal's life as a gift from God. As such, God is violated when the lives of his creatures are perverted. This translates into stewardship and respect of animals, rather than domination and exploitation.

Some people in China claim that eating dog meat helps keep the human body warm in winter. This antiquated custom grates on the fast-emerging modern middle class that has grown fond of dogs as companions – and not as food fare. This new type of thinking no doubt creates conflict with older and poorer generations. A proposed new law – to outlaw the consumption and sale of dog meat – has provoked fiery debate, with many Chinese vociferously defending dog eating as a

Animals in our care deserve to be treated humanely, with compassion and dignity during their lifetime.

time-honoured tradition of their culture. Increasing criticism from western society and its growing influence on their values remain contentious issues.

In the west, we cringe to imagine the short, wretched lives of caged dogs destined for the food industry, and quickly condemn eastern values. How can we take such a stance yet still allow the slaughter of another animal considered a companion by many – the horse? While we may not have a taste for horsemeat here in North America, it is accepted as an alternative to beef in Europe and Asia. And so lame, old, and sometimes even "excess" horses are sent to processing facilities, and their meat shipped to other parts of the world.

Does this not give us pause? Most of us eat some type of meat for sustenance. And we probably wear or use products made from the hides of animals. In fact, we have evolved, survived and thrived as humans by consuming other animals – so how can we deem it wrong? When we get down to the heart of the issue, does it really matter whether animals

are domesticated or wild, companions or stock? Whether they are dogs, horses, cows, chickens or deer? Do we decide which are eligible to become "consumables" solely by how our culture feels about them? Or by how we react emotionally as individuals? Indeed, living in this world without *any* inconsistency in our views and treatment of animals is nearly impossible. Perhaps what matters most, and what we should all agree on, is that animals in our care – whether for consumption or not – deserve to be treated humanely, with compassion and dignity during their lifetime. And especially at the end of their lives.

An Accident of Birth

Jenna is one of the caring souls that offer a promise of better lives for these dogs. Wearing traditional handmade beaded suede-and-fur moccasins, she greets us in front of her house, proudly lifting this 12-week old puppy to show us what a beautiful boy he is. But while she loves her gentle blond female dog and her progeny, Jenna admits she is overwhelmed with feeding and finding homes for these puppies. She's doing her best to look after them all, but she simply does not have the resources to deal with the endless unwanted pregnancies.

Jenna listens intently as we explain the procedure and its benefits, and quickly accepts the offer to have her companion dog implanted with a contraceptive. Happy to be relieved of her ongoing burden, she tries to help in any way she can, chasing, grabbing, and lifting each puppy by its front legs so we can identify its gender (not only is the sex of each puppy apparent, but also how bloated and wormy its bulging little belly is). She sees the contraceptive as a blessing for her female dog, providing the birth control she needs and so desires.

She also agrees to relinquish all the puppies for adoption except one – another little blond female – that we implant in the same fashion as her mother.

For many First Nations people, the burgeoning number of unwanted dogs on their reserves is clearly a problem, and they welcome any help, whether surgical sterilization or medical contraception, to manage it. But not all agree. Some think we should allow the dogs to live out their lives, however they might unfold. Some believe we are showing disrespect to the nature of dogs when we spay or neuter. The contraceptive implant, because it does not alter the dog in any obvious way physically, is an option that many accept in good grace. Even within a single culture, differing opinions prevail on the welfare and husbandry of the dogs but all people who live there feel the repercussions.

In traditional Native American culture, the spiritual belief system is composed of circles and cycles, and promotes balance and harmony among physical and spiritual elements. The central tenet, "God is within all things," emphasizes the interconnectedness of all life forms and respect for Mother Earth and her creatures. Animals have long been viewed as teachers and guides, a way to communicate with the Creator or "Great Spirit." In days past, the very existence of Native Americans was dependent upon animals for food, clothing, shelter, and transportation; as such, animals were respected and honoured. Although they weren't worshipped, they did hold symbolic powers. "Power animals" possessed characteristics and strengths that were adopted by entire families or tribes who held similar human attributes. Nine different animals were deemed guardian spirits, and called upon when spiritual assistance was required for difficult stages of a life journey. Close relatives of the dog – the wolf and

the coyote – were included, whereas the dog itself was simply a part of everyday events.

The Native American way of life in the era before horses became reliable workmates is sometimes referred to as their "dog culture." Dogs were valued members of the tribe – as companions, hunting and tracking game, and even as a consumable food source when necessary. They hauled supplies and belongings – even children and the elderly – as they pulled the famous travois across the plains. Dogs warned the tribe of approaching enemies or visitors, and protected the most vulnerable family members when the men were away hunting and the women were off gathering roots, berries and herbs.

Notably, history tells us that dogs were plentiful and, even then, enjoyed the freedom to roam. They bred freely with little selective control by humans, apart from the culling of sick pups and those with poor dispositions. Some pups were also destroyed to ease the nursing burden on the bitch; the survivors were probably selected for their preferred physical characteristics. Perhaps that was enough to keep populations in relative check.

Anecdotal interpretations by early explorers describe "Indian dogs" as being almost impossible to distinguish from wolves. The northern tribes developed larger dogs with wolf-like characteristics that would better withstand colder climates. In fact, many types of dogs – as diverse and unique as the people with whom they inhabited the land – co-existed with indigenous groups, and were used for a variety of purposes.

Unfortunately, the traditional lifestyle of Native Americans – with its pure simplicity and strong connection to nature – began to disintegrate with the invasion of the white man. The territorial exclusion, extermination of buffalo, and formation of reserves that followed the Europeans' arrival created social problems that have irrevocably changed the lives of indigenous people. Dogs, innocent bystanders of such cultural drift, lost much of their status and purpose as working members of the tribe. In the years since, surplus dogs have been left to fend for themselves – sometimes rewarded with a helping hand, at other times with a cruel blow.

Why Value the Valueless?

Jack is one of our unsung heroes for these homeless dogs with no names. Without fail, he has driven out to the rez every week to feed them, except for the stretch three years ago while he was recuperating from a heart attack. That was his only miss in a decade. An impromptu visit inside this abandoned house to investigate a crying puppy reveals Jack's dedication to his thankless, self-imposed task of the last ten years. At least four adult feral dogs have been using this building to escape the weather and help themselves to the food Jack leaves behind. We discover tell-tale evidence that females have given birth here too, though all we find this day is a lone survivor.

Once, Jack made it a habit to remove all the old boxes and torn food bags, but as age has taken its toll, he's started to measure his energy expenditures more carefully. Understandably, he prefers to expand his efforts carrying thirty-pound bags of dog food up the stairs and into the house, rather than taxing himself hauling out stacks of paper and cardboard waste. Jack has asked the people that live "a stone's throw away" to help these timid dogs a little by setting a bucket of fresh water outside once in a while. Some do, he says, and some don't.

A dog with no name has no financial value: no one will pay to acquire him. Nor does he have any value emotionally: no one is agonizing over his loss or looking for him. If the animal has no worth to society, why then do we tolerate his presence? We don't really; we only tolerate him if he remains invisible. In most urban areas, if a stray becomes troublesome, he is picked up by animal control services. But out on the reserve, he has miles to wander, and as long as his behaviour remains submissive and non-threatening, he is likely to be left alone.

People spend hundreds – even thousands – of dollars for a dog from a pet store or "breeder." Often the dog has no pedigree; he may be a "designer" dog, such as a Malador or Puggle. Why does such a dog command a high dollar value while a dog with no name has none? Unfortunately, the value attributed to a dog does not reflect the animal's intrinsic worth, either individually or as a species. Instead, dollar value is a reflection of current trends, popular demand and, finally, the emotional needs of the person making the purchase.

Of paramount importance is how the dog makes the owner feel, much like any "product" chosen for looks or prestige. Indeed, a person who acquires a purebred or crossbred dog at considerable cost – other than for specific working purposes such as herding, guarding, or hunting (though perhaps those dogs should be included too) – may be seeking to define self through the dog's perceived image, or through social activities associated with the dog. Think Chihuahua – loving companion and fashion accessory, all in one tidy little package.

Granted, a person with a love of animals may desire an outlet for this love, and a dog in need of a home

– whether or not it has a special label or pedigree – will more than fulfill that need. Sure, we can argue that the physical traits and disposition of a purebred or specialty dog are more defined and reliable than those of a dog with unknown parentage; that is certainly true when dealing with responsible breeders. With the prevalence of puppy mills and Internet sales, however, even those physical factors are difficult to discern.

Why should we value a nameless dog when it seems to have no value? The answers are both simple and profound. To enrich our existence with greater meaning and depth. To discourage the proliferation of puppy factories. And to give a vulnerable animal the life it surely deserves.

...When does our sense of compassion give way to our sense of self-preservation, especially in the face of defeat?

The Best of Intentions

On reserve land, a yard surrounded by fencing is an unusual sight; so is an on-site dog kennel. This resident was trying hard to limit the breeding of his two female mastiff-type dogs. He might have achieved some success, if not for the hundreds of male dogs roaming freely. Unfortunately, all he accomplished was to limit the freedom of his own captive dogs. Male dogs can smell pheromones of females in heat from great distances. And these determined fellows are unstoppable; they will jump fences and dig under pens to breed receptive female dogs, especially ones – like the sad-eyed girl in the photograph – that are unable to escape. The owner's good intentions certainly kept his dogs safe from mortal perils. But as a method of birth control, it was a lost cause.

As you can see, this dejected female looks defeated by life; unfortunately, so did her owner. While he was trying to do the right thing, the birth of multiple puppies suggested he had come up short in achieving his goal. To any outsider, the obvious solution would be to have the dogs spayed. However, like many "owned" dogs on the rez, these two had probably never travelled in a vehicle; they were fearful of firm restraint, and crate confinement seemed out of the question. One was advanced in age, with less-than-ideal body condition; overall, they were poor candidates for hospitalization and surgical sterilization. The best solution here was to implant each of them with a contraceptive, thereby giving them a respite from reproduction. This turned out to be no trouble at all: in their familiar environment, we found them to be gentle and receptive, accustomed to a kind human touch.

The owner had obviously been through a frustrating time. No matter what he did to shield his females from being bred, he simply could not barricade them from the male dogs – some neighbour-owned, others feral – that ran loose on reserve land. He was no doubt wondering, as most of us surely would, how close to his breaking point he had come. Indeed, when does our sense of compassion give way to our sense of self-preservation, especially in the face of defeat? We can certainly understand how apathy can take hold in such a hopeless situation. So why do we keep on trying?

If we are to live in harmony with others, as well as

ourselves, every moral decision we make requires that other beings are taken into account. Our subconscious brain is always driven to balance self-preservation (selfishness) against altruism (selflessness). This very delicate balancing act is in constant need of nurturing as we navigate through life's many obstacles. But the search for balance is precisely what gives our lives meaning and dignity.

For the months ahead, at least, these two gentle dogs will enjoy a reprieve from persistent male dogs and burdensome pregnancies.

If we are to live in harmony with others, as well as ourselves, every moral decision we make requires that other beings are taken into account.

A Helping Hand

On a chilly January day, this doghouse was delivered to the rez. Whoever placed it there had thoughtfully angled it southward, to catch the warmth of the winter sun and block the cold north wind from blowing inside. To the right of the doghouse, was the remnant of a trail pounded into the snow by dogs also seeking shelter in the abandoned vehicles. These dogs take cover wherever they can; inside and underneath cars are among their favourite hideaways. In inclement weather, alas, there is never enough shelter to go around.

Some very kind people live on this earth, and some of them are heaven sent. This doghouse, along with several others, came as a gift from the owner of an art gallery. While removing art pieces from shipping crates, she came up with a brainstorm: why not recycle the boxes as shelter? So she commissioned a carpenter to build insulated doghouses from the discarded wood. The doghouses, each imprinted with the logo of a local rescue group, are provided to residents trying to improve the lives of rez dogs.

When he saw the idea put into action by the compassionate gallery owner (Angel 1), Angel 2 formulated his own plan. Bob, an 82-year-old retired plumber suffering from Parkinson's disease, began retrieving discarded building scraps from houses under construction to build even more doghouses. The rez dogs now use every doghouse built by these two. Angel 1 and Angel 2, we salute you!

Muhammad Ali said, "Service to others is the rent you pay for your room here on earth." But there is much more to it than that. Ideally, we offer service to others simply because others exist and have unfulfilled needs. Behaving with unselfish regard for others, however, doesn't always come naturally (though some psychologists believe empathy is hardwired into us, a carryover from ancestral days when cooperative behaviour assured survival in harsh conditions). Most of us agree that when we give of ourselves, without expectations of reciprocity, we feel both fulfilled and energized. True soul-satisfying service is a gift we give not only to others, but also to ourselves.

True soul-satisfying service is a gift we give not only to others,
but also to ourselves.

Hurt but Safe

On first impression, this big male dog looks like a brute of a fellow, but the presence of a cat relaxing nearby on a ratty old armchair indicates otherwise.

We first see him on a frigid -17C winter's day made even colder by ice crystals whipping in the wind; he's one of seven dogs hanging around this house,

all behaving calmly. They're obviously not starving, and the freezing temperatures help keep them docile. None of them pay any attention to the numerous cats perched on fence railings and abandoned car tires, soaking up the feeble rays of a January sun. This large dog moves as though in slow motion, his left foot markedly swollen with hair missing around the toes. His injury is likely the result of trauma, perhaps a bite wound or laceration from some type of sharp object. At sub-zero temperatures, unprotected wounds heal very slowly, with the scaffold of new cells and fragile skin layers repeating an endless cycle of freezing and dying. On the upside, open wounds hardly ever get infected, as pus formation is also impeded and the absence of flies keeps the sores free of irritation. Injured or not, this male dog won't allow anyone near him, let alone close enough to catch him. Resolutely shy, he maintains a constant distance of five to six paces from us, tail down, ears erect, but never a lip curl.

Meeting the occupant of the house, we are heartened by what he reveals: he is empathetic to the plight of dogs and cats with no names, and has resolved to use his allotted land on the reserve as a haven for any four-legged animals that come his way. People in the area have come to know this, and he sometimes discovers cardboard boxes filled with young litters of kittens or puppies at the end of his gravel driveway. He always takes them in. As much as he might like to, he can't afford any medical or surgical treatment for any of the strays (and he truly appreciates the assistance a local rescue group provides). But he does the best he can: he feeds them all, tucks straw bedding into the five derelict cars in the yard, and leaves old pieces of furniture outside as additional shelter for them. Under his deck are two makeshift doghouses. On a warm day, the smell of urine and excrement is enough to take your breath away, but what do the animals care? They are safe, fed and, above all, loved – and for that they are grateful.

"At times our own light goes out and is rekindled by a spark from another person. Each of us has cause to think with deep gratitude of those who have lighted the flame within us."

– Albert Schweitzer

A Candle in the Night

Rain or shine, in scorching heat or bitter cold, Jack is out on the rez doing his lonely tours of duty. He has bonded with people who appreciate his dedicated efforts with sick and dying dogs, by rescuing them and seeking medical help for them. But not every local rolls out the welcome mat. Jack has also has been vilified for establishing feeding stations for the dogs: some see his benevolent activities as perpetuating the problem, instead of letting nature take its course. Jack walks a fine line by helping unwanted dogs; fortunately, at his age, he has the wisdom and grace to tread softly. Jack, we salute you!

But this gentle senior is also a realist: he knows he cannot save every stray dog. "You would do this dog a favour by shooting it," Jack says softly as he looks over one ailing animal. The day is frigid, -20C, with snow on the ground, when we come upon the poor fellow. The dog's face is full of porcupine quills, with pus oozing from his half-closed eyes. He is feral, we can see that – but he's also deathly ill, and can only gather enough strength to *try* to run away from us.

"He can no longer eat, you can see his ribs, and he is starving – he'll die from the cold," Jack tells us sadly, "You definitely would do him a favour by shooting him."

Even so, giving up has always been a last resort for Jack: he somehow manages to catch the frail dog and bring him to the clinic.

Humpback whales are the largest mammals on the planet; their hearts are the size of a Volkswagen beetle. But Jack's heart is surely bigger. Ten years ago, Jack was selling vehicles on the reserve. He started to bring dog food along on his visits, to feed the thin dogs he encountered along the roads and ditches. Ten years later, Jack is retired but still visits the reserve several times a week to deliver dog food to the many famished, wandering dogs. Jack is in his 80s now, though you would never know it to look at him.

"It is hopeless," Jack concedes, "If you look at the big picture, it's a losing battle." But somehow he does not sound discouraged.

"On this reserve alone, there must be at least a thousand dogs," he tells us, "And less than 20 per cent have a name, much less are fed and given some comfort like shelter. Worse, we've taken away most of their hunting abilities, so they're all scavengers and beggars. I saw Blue-Eyes (a short-haired, medium-sized dog with striking blue eyes like a husky's) feeding on something in the ditch. Turns out he was gnawing away on his dead sister – she likely got hit by a car. But what's he to do? He's hungry!"

"Some Natives hunt deer on the reserve for their own consumption and leave the carcass for the dogs to finish off. But the dogs have to fight the coyotes off the carcass first. *If* these dogs could get enough food and water, some shelter to keep the cold away, and a little pat on

Feeding hungry dogs is not for the faint of heart.

the head once in awhile to say 'hi there' – it might be a good life, roaming around with no obligations!"

But the *if* is too big to ever be fulfilled. And Jack knows it.

"The dump is where you see the desperation of these hungry dogs," he tells us, "If a timid dog finds a piece of food worth eating and other dogs are nearby, they'll come over and attack him so he drops the piece of food. If he doesn't, he might be killed for it. These dogs don't live more than a couple years, if they even last that long."

"And winter is really tough on the dogs, especially the females and their pups."

In the spring and summer, dogs often find water in ditches and puddles, but by late summer much of that supply has dried up. And by winter, all the natural water sources are frozen solid. For a lactating female, eating enough snow to produce milk for 6 to 10 puppies is tough, sometimes impossible.

"When she weans the surviving puppies, these little guys don't know where to look for water. Or they get worn out wandering long distances in search of it.

They die of dehydration."

"I have a letter from the Band Chief to allow me to drive around and feed the dogs. I understand some Natives not liking me. I've been yelled at more than once: 'Hey you, white man, I'll call the police if you come near my house to feed the dogs!' I get it – I'd be unhappy if a Native came to my neighbourhood with a letter from the mayor allowing him to come and feed squirrels. What I don't understand, though, is how some Natives can abandon their dogs… but then, some white people do that too. Their attitude is, 'I look after myself, so you look after yourself, too.' It's not done with the intention of being mean – it's just the way it is."

"Dogs get hungry and form packs. I don't feed dogs in packs," Jack admits, "It's too dangerous. They go crazy for the food and start attacking each other, or start going after me. So sometimes what I do is drive slowly and throw food out my van window. That way I'm protected, and the food is spread far enough away that the frenzied dogs have some distance between them and don't attack one another. I can understand that Natives with young children get nervous with dogs roaming in packs – they feel it's unsafe to leave their children outdoors. Then someone has to go and shoot the dogs to break up the packs."

"I think the saddest thing is to see a female in a hole under a tree, surrounded by frozen puppies in the snow." He pauses, and the image lingers. "Am I making a difference by feeding these dogs? Probably not… in ten years, it still seems to be the same. But what am I going to do, stay home and watch TV? For the individual dog, it *has* made a difference. But the big picture probably hasn't changed much."

"I will keep doing this," Jack says quietly, "Until I cross the great divide."

For these homeless animals, Jack is a candle in the night that chases the darkness away.

His Territory

This black male was hunkered down under an old abandoned truck for shelter and safety, oblivious to the inscription on the license plate above his head: "Indian and Proud of it!" Yet the words accurately

> "To man, freedom is another word for nothing left to lose;
> to a dog, it is a synonym for despair."
>
> – Author Unknown

define who he is, at least in the eyes of most people that happen by his crude shelter. There is no doubt that he belongs to a category, though not of his own making. Placid but vigilant, this hardy outdoor dog is completely unaware that his lot in life is worlds away from that of our precious and pampered companion dogs. But like all *Canis lupus familiaris*,

he is genetically wired to move and to expand energy, thanks to his wolf ancestry. As a rez dog he complies with his basic urges: to roam, breed and feed. To him, life is slow and short. He has no concept of what's fair and what isn't, in his life or anyone else's.

While he may seem unique as a dog scratching

out a living on a First Nations reserve, his fate is unfortunately shared by dogs the world over. Dogs with no names struggle for survival in the rural landscapes of almost every country, on the crowded streets of sprawling urban areas and within decaying city centers. They are the unwanted, the excess, the wandering dogs that – through no fault of their own – are birthed into uncertain, difficult, often brief lives. And despite high mortality rates, their numbers persist. Indeed, the sheer number of these dogs guarantees that sufficient progeny survive long enough to propagate another cycle of misery. And yet another.

As human beings, our innate sense of decency and compassion – beyond kindness and good intentions – should unite us in our treatment of animals; especially dogs who are our oldest and most loyal companions. Dogs are unmistakably our creations, the products of our needs, whims and desires. Witness the evidence – intensive genetic sculpting, a little social stupidity – and how can we deny it? Deliberately crafted to be dependent upon us, dogs barely have a life worth living when humankind fails to stand by their side. This fact alone should cement the foundation of our two-way social contract with canines. And if the contract were truly fair, it would also demand our expressed moral concern for these vulnerable creatures. Bernard Rollin a famed ethicist expressed it best when he stated that kindness and good intent do not assure moral treatment – moral concern does.

ourselves as a species? Or have we forgotten that we, too, are part of the animal world – and in forgetting, have we become too far removed from its reality and its truths?

...kindness and good intent do not assure moral treatment –
moral concern does.

If we, as human beings, have difficulty relating to other life forms and the pain and suffering we inflict upon them (whether deliberately or through ignorance), perhaps this failure points to our own shortcomings. Do we fail others because we have not yet defined

Perhaps by acknowledging the basic right of animals to live life in accordance with its nature, we would appease our moral ambiguity about our paradoxical relationships with them. In the meantime, finding our common ground in terms of humane treatment

– of not only dogs, but also all animals – and putting that humanity into practice would transcend any geographical border, religious belief, cultural tradition or personal opinion. And would not such an effort bring us all greater peace?

After all, death is not the worst thing that can happen to an animal. But a lifetime of fear and suffering just might be.

The 100th Dog

"Life is just one damned thing after another."

– Elbert Hubbard

"It is not true that life is one damn thing after another;
it is one damn thing over and over."

– Edna St-Vincent Millay

Life is one damn thing over and over, and we should be grateful for that. What if our hearts got tired of beating the same way (72 times per minute, or over 100,000 times per day), and decided to beat in slow motion or to the rhythm of jazz? What if our lungs entertained the thought of not exchanging oxygen and carbon dioxide in the same alveoli with reliable regularity during our sleeping hours? Physiologically, it is a blessing that one damn thing occurs over and over in our bodies. Indeed, if we could rely on this impeccable constancy long term, aging – with all its accompanying foes, such as organ degeneration and cancer – would never happen.

Emotionally and spiritually, however, doing the same thing over and over is clearly a paradox for us as humans. A life of repetition can bring both drudgery and joy. When we insist on repeating actions and words that cause us heartaches and headaches, we immerse ourselves in self-imposed drudgery. Some (if not all) of us excel at replicating the same transgressions, the same sins, and the same acts that invariably bring forth sorrow and misery. Often we do this with the belief – and the hope – that life will unfold with some randomness, and that our repeated patterns, however miserable they make us feel, might not roll out exactly the same outcomes as in the past.

Maybe sheer laziness or stubborn refusal to change our ways explains why we persist in efforts to reduce our lives to one damn thing over and over.

Does such a pattern serve any purpose? Without a certain amount of wishful repetition, our lives would no doubt be totally dysfunctional. Imagine how long it would take to devise new ways to perform daily tasks, such as doing the laundry or making beds! For the sake of efficiency and speed, we have learned it is best to rely on established neuronal pathways. The major drawback of such willful repetition? Boredom inevitably sets in, and with it comes a cloud of mediocrity that grows and wraps itself around our thoughts and actions. The only way to truly break free of this tedious, vicious circle is through well-timed, self-imposed challenges, colored with the motivation to excel and create.

On the other paw, we know it is at times impossible to avoid performing the same damn thing over and over. Implanting 100 female rez dogs with contraceptives requires us to insert 100 contraceptive implants, in the same subcutaneous neck area, 100 times. There is no way around it. (Or perhaps there is. All 100 female rez dogs could be surgically altered, a prohibitively labor- and time-intensive process that also calls for repeated precision. Not a great alternative.)

Of this we remind ourselves: repetition can be a joy if and only if our actions are carried out with love and intent while being in the present moment and nowhere else. If each female rez dog we implant has our exclusive attention and full awareness, and receives all the care and comfort that love can provide, then we accomplish the same damn thing over and over with pleasure and satisfaction.

Conclusion

To travel a path of hopelessness and apathy is not how anyone's journey on this earth is meant to unfold.

Another Sunset

When we set out on this journey, our goal was simply to implant a study group of 100 dogs with contraceptives. Preventing lives of misery was our main objective. To achieve this, we had to prevent pregnancies and pre-empt the birth of unwanted litters. But what we realized from our efforts was that while our experiences brought us great joy and fulfillment, they also brought profound sadness and disappointment. Indeed, the challenges of working with these nameless dogs reminded us time and again how overwhelming the world and its complexities can be. Through a deeper understanding of the lives lived on reserves, a number of reflections, rationalizations and resolutions came to light. The most obvious one?

In the end, being engaged in acts of selfless love helps each of us to preserve our own sanity.

To travel a path of hopelessness and apathy is not how anyone's journey on this earth is meant to unfold. We all need to give and receive love, understanding and comfort; we need a reason to remain rational in the face of all of the adversity in our lives. The reserve dogs taught us profound lessons. They showed us by example that a life well lived is far more than "just getting by." They showed us how to celebrate our lives to the fullest – even as we accept the uncertainty and randomness of each day.

What drives us to pretend that the tragedies of the world do not exist, or do not affect us? As human beings, we deny ourselves the truth of what it means to be alive when we fail to recognize the conflicts within, or refuse to resolve them. The key to a deeper sense of peace and tranquility is not in dodging the harsh reality of life, but in embracing it – truly getting in touch and moving through it.

Too soon our journey ends: as a day once clear and bright draws to a close, our work with the dogs winds down to its final reel. Around us, the shadows lengthen and temperatures drop. But still we linger,

enjoying the serenity, the beauty of the land. Then, finally, the time comes to pack up and organize the van for our trip back to town. As usual, we empty the last bags of kibble onto the ground to feed hungry pups that might wander by after our departure. Taking a last look around for signs of canine life, we notice a dark shape inside a nearby car wreck. The snow has softened over the afternoon and slithered down the window, revealing a large dog sitting tall behind the steering wheel, right there in the driver's seat. He's likely known all along we were there, but he's trying his best to avoid eye contact. No doubt he is somewhat fearful, but there's more to it than that: he's probably cold, and any movement means losing precious body heat. We observe him from afar as he leans in close to the window, intent on absorbing the last tepid rays of the waning winter sun before it drops behind the mountain peaks. All is quiet then, except for the soft wing beats of a raven flying west. And for a surreal moment, time stands still.

...live as though the world is already better than you think.

In that moment, we became aware. This dog – this

perfect, unspoiled being – is showing us the simple, peaceful reality that has been eluding us all along: live as though the world is already better than you think. Invest in it all the goodness you possess and can offer.

On behalf of all dogs with no names, wherever they may be, thank you from the bottom of my heart.

Judith Samson-French

Photo Credits

For having seized the moment and freely contributing their photographs, thank you.

Julie Bousfield: p 18

Marg Chadder: p 222

Susan Chen: p 44

Evocative Photography: pp 2, 5, 6, 8, 13, 15, 20, 24, 30, 39, 47, 50, 64, 69, 71, 80, 83, 93, 95, 96, 98, 101, 111, 112, 115, 120, 150, 152, 168, 170, 176, 188, 203, 213, 217, 233, 236, 239, 243, 247, 251, 262, 265, 271, 275, 279, 280, 285, 286, 291, 293, 297, 299

Julie Felber: p 288

Kim French: pp 41, 122, 125, 127, 128, 131, 132, 136, 139, 141, 180, 209, 211

Susanne Imorde: p 142

Lindsay Morgenstern: pp 35, 106

Tanya Reid: pp 53, 138, 160,

Lori Rogers: p 90

Judith Samson-French: pp 23, 26, 29, 32, 48, 52, 56, 60, 66, 72, 76, 84, 85, 86, 103, 116, 119, 146, 156, 158, 164, 171, 173, 185, 190, 193, 194, 198, 204, 221, 225, 248, 254, 258, 268, 295

Acknowledgements

Dogs with no names are masters of hope and forgiveness; they are also superb teachers. For revealing a world of controlled fear, patience, acceptance, and heartfelt tail-wagging joy when handled, I am deeply grateful to them. To all First Nations community members who welcomed our efforts and helped me see and understand the challenges of the dog overpopulation problem, I extend a generous thank you.

This book is a reflection of a scientific project in progress, and its advancement has only been made possible due to the motivation and hard work of a dedicated team of people. Lori Rogers provided incredible momentum, Julie Felber dedication, Mona Jorgenson tenacity, and Erica and James Fernandes' truly Evocative Photography.

I would especially like to thank Sue Tompkins, Dr. Daphne Barnes, Dr. Susanne Imorde, Alex Bogner, Dorris Heffron, and Lindsay Morgenstern for their insights and their gifts of time. Patricia Conrad deserves gratitude for editing this manuscript with much patience, enthusiasm and generosity. I am indebted to Jack Glaser, who in his ninth decade of life continues to selflessly help some of the most disenfranchised animals – he is truly a candle in the night. Tanya Reid is warmly acknowledged for her creative contribution and Sue Impey as graphic designer extraordinaire.

Finally, I must deeply thank my husband Kim and my son Erik Jorgenson, for their unwavering support and for so warmly embracing the dogs with no names in our lives.

About the Author

An experienced veterinary clinician and surgeon with over 20 years of experience, Dr. Judith Samson-French owns and operates a veterinary hospital in the heart of the beautiful Rocky Mountain foothills. Dr. Samson-French acquired a BSc from McGill University and a MSc from the University of Alberta by completing a thesis on lungworm pneumonia in bighorn sheep. She received her doctorate in veterinary medicine from the Ontario Veterinary College.

Dr. Samson-French's experience with animals is multi-layered and diverse: she has worked at both the Calgary Zoo and the Honolulu Zoo, she has worked as an emergency veterinarian as well as a general practitioner, she has invested several years of her career to pursuing medicine and surgery for ratites (ostriches, emus, and rheas) in North America and Europe, and has pursued education in aquatic veterinary medicine, studying at the Woods Hole Oceanographic Institute and Bamfield Marine Station in western Canada.

She is currently leading a first-time trial project that involves implanting contraceptives in unwanted dogs on Native reserve land adjacent to her veterinary facility to prevent the potential births of 100,000's dogs with no names.

She lives in Bragg Creek with her husband Kimberley French, her son Erik, two dogs and six donkeys. They have no cats.

Please visit us at dogswithnonames.ca

Selected Bibliography

Bauer Nona K. Dog Heroes of September 11th: A Tribute to America's Search and Rescue Dogs. New Jersey: Kennel Club Books, 2011.

Grandin T., and. Johnson C. Animals in Translation: Using the Mysteries of Autism to Decode Animals' Behavior. Florida: Harcourt, 2005.

Herzog Hal. Some We Love, Some We Hate, Some We Eat: Why It's So Hard To Think Straight About Animals. New York: HarperCollins Publishers, 2010.

Horowitz Alexandra. Inside of a Dog: What Dogs See, Smell, and Know. New York: Scribner, 2009.

Masson J.M., and Wolfe A. Dogs Make Us Human: A Global Family Album. New York: Bloomsbury, 2011.

Osho. The Book of Wisdom. New York: Osho Media International, 2009.

Rollin Bernard E. Animal Rights & Human Morality. New York: Prometheus Books, 2006.

Schweitzer Albert. Reverence for Life: The Words of Albert Schweitzer. New York: HarperCollins Publishers, 1993.

Singer Peter. Practical Ethics. New York: Cambridge University Press, 1993.